Cleopatra

The life and loves of the world's most powerful woman

Elizabeth Benchley

Astrolog Publishing House

Language Consultant: Jody Bar-On

Cover Design: Na'ama Yaffe
Layout and Graphics: Daniel Akerman
Production Manager: Dan Gold

P.O. Box 1123, Hod Hasharon 45111, Israel
Tel: 972-9-7412044
Fax: 972-9-7442714

© Astrolog Publishing House Ltd. 2004

ISBN 965-494-145-7

Published by Astrolog Publishing House 2004

10 9 8 7 6 5 4 3 2 1

Timeline

69 B.C.	Birth of Cleopatra
48 B.C.	Caesar restores Cleopatra on the Egyptian throne
46-44 B.C.	Cleopatra resides in Rome
44-40 B.C.	Elimination of Caesar's assassins
44 B.C.	Assassination of Caesar
43 B.C.	Formation of the triumvirate: Antony - Octavian (Augustus) - Lepidus
43-42 B.C.	Victory of the triumvirate over Caesar's assassins at Philippi Antony in charge of reorganizing the Orient
42 B.C.	Dionysiac entry of Antony at Ephesus
41 B.C.	Meeting between Antony and Cleopatra at Tarsus
40-34 B.C.	Formation of the two blocks
40 B.C.	Treaty between Antony, Octavian, and Lepidus
36 B.C.	Elimination of Lepidus Octavian controls Africa and becomes the effective ruler of Rome Parthian campaign of Marc Antony
34 B.C.	Organization of the "Antonian Orient"
32 B.C.	Western provinces pledge allegiance to Octavian Declaration of war on Cleopatra Antony and his allies gather on the Island of Samos
31 B.C.	Battle of Actium and victory of Octavian Antony and Cleopatra seek refuge at Alexandria
30 B.C.	Victory of Octavian at Alexandria Suicide of Antony and Cleopatra Egypt becomes a Roman province

On August 10, in the year 30 B.C., the body of Cleopatra VII, The last Egyptian Pharaoh, was found in a mausoleum she had built for herself in Alexandria. Cleopatra had taken her own life at thirty-nine years of age. We shall probably never be certain with exactly what means she accomplished this, her last dramatic feat. However, much is known about the tumultuous, passionate, remarkable life that preceded it, and which, perhaps, made it inevitable. Cleopatra the Great left questions that have occupied the minds of generations since antiquity. Who was this enigmatic woman? By what talents and designs did she manage to influence the most powerful men the world had ever known, and to alter the course of history? To begin to understand we must delve deep into ancient times, and examine the roots and fertile ground from which the amazing Queen arose.

• Made in Greece •

When the Macedonian conqueror Alexander the Great died in 331 B.C., he left behind no natural legitimate heir. Military administration of his far-reaching empire was divided among his generals. Ptolemy, son of Lagus, a Macedonian Greek, was a companion and advisor to Alexander who had recently been promoted to rank of general and entrusted with various military responsibilities. Ptolemy was not interested in controlling an empire and had never subscribed to Alexander's expansionist vision. He shrewdly opted out of the intense power struggle among the generals and undertook administrative control of Egypt, a wealthy and independent, although fairly isolated land, along with Libya and Arabia.

The man who would become the first Ptolemy Pharaoh was a man of contemplation and careful thought as well as of ambition and decisive action. His political astuteness and his personal ambition combined to make him a successful ruler. Ptolemy I contrived to have the body of Alexander laid to rest in Egypt, rather than in Macedonia, lending himself an air of identification with the great man.

When Ptolemy I declared himself King of Egypt in 304 B.C., the 300-year rule of the Ptolemaic Pharaohs began. The city of Alexandria was the seat of the monarchy, and thrived and grew during his rule. The great Library of Alexandria was conceived and built during the reign of the first Pharaoh as were many other state buildings and structures. Ptolemy I oversaw and encouraged the immense intellectual and cultural growth of the city.

Ptolemy I

King Ptolemy I had several wives and many children. His third wife, Berenice, became original mother of the dynasty, as Ptolemy appointed his son by her his heir, even though he had older children by a previous wife. Historical conjecture holds that Berenice was in fact Ptolemy's full sister. If so, this began an almost ironclad family tradition by which most of the marriages in subsequent generations of Ptolemies were clearly incestuous in the first degree. Berenice was herself a forceful figure and a powerful woman who probably influenced the rule of Egypt as much as her brother/husband. Their son, Ptolemy II Philadelphus stepped up to the throne when at last at age 82, Ptolemy I stepped down.

Ptolemy II, a lover of art and poetry, and possessed of many positive personal characteristics, was by all accounts well respected and liked. A man of contradictions, however, he did on occasion demonstrate the fiery Ptolemy will and he certainly had a love of power. The second Ptolemy established a thriving court life in Alexandria, and continued his father's patronage of the arts and sciences. The great library doubled its holdings and was cataloged under his direction. Ptolemy II, like his father before him, placed great importance on the capital, and continued to expand and maintain the great city of Alexandria. Militarily, Egypt held its own in

Ptolemy II

the region and was secure as a powerful force to be reckoned with. Ptolemy II married his half-sister, Arsinoe, and she bore him a son, Ptolemy III. He later married a second Arsinoe, his full natural sister, and remained in that marriage until the latter passed away. It is said that this sibling marriage was also a true love relationship and that Ptolemy II mourned long for his sister-wife after her death. Numerous temples and statues in Alexandria were constructed in her memory, and she was worshipped along with the Egyptian gods.

Ptolemy III

The second Arsinoe had adopted her nephew/stepson Ptolemy III, and he was named heir to the throne. Ptolemy III married his sister Berenice, and ruled Egypt until 221 B.C., overseeing a great era in Egypt's history. This Ptolemy was perhaps less intelligent and astute than his predecessors, but he succeeded militarily and expanded Egypt's influence, especially to the east. Alexandria continued to flourish, and the country was wealthy and militarily secure.

Under the reign of the first three Ptolemaic rulers, Alexandria and Egypt experienced a golden age of growth and achievement. Alexandria was probably the largest city in the world, and definitely an intellectual and scientific center of great importance. The construction of the great palace of the Pharaohs took place during this time, and important agricultural and educational strides were made. The Alexandrian School was established and populated by numerous Hellenist Greek scholars. The library and museum attracted notable scholars as well, although no particular new discoveries or philosophies are traced to this period.

Things winds of change began to blow strongly after Ptolemy III.

While the tradition of incestuous marriage began right at the outset of the Ptolemaic dynasty, the first three demonstrated at least a modicum of personal integrity. After that, the descent of the family into depravity, cruelty and greed became more pronounced with each succeeding Ptolemaic ruler. Murder of siblings, parents and children became as common as marriage among the same. When Ptolemy IV, son of Ptolemy III and Berenice came of age, a Ptolemy "bad seed" seemed to have emerged. Some believe that the inbreeding practiced by the clan had begun to cause the decline of its better attributes and the passing down of the more vicious and unsavory of human tendencies.

It is believed that Ptolemy III was murdered by his young son who was impatient to achieve the throne. Ptolemy IV then began his reign over Egypt with a sickening string of further murders that wiped out most of his remaining family, including his brother and mother. He married his sister, another Arsinoe, but was known to consort with both men and women of the court. This Ptolemy completely disregarded the Greek tradition of respect for family ties and regard for one's elders, and simply ran rampant over anyone and everyone whom he perceived as any kind of threat. His life style was one of low pursuits, and he often entertained young boy prostitutes and a circle of various mistresses. Many of his closest advisors were known criminals. When he died, his wife, Arsinoe III was to become Queen, but her dead husband's ministers had her put to death, and her son, Ptolemy V, then still a child, was put on the throne.

The Ptolemy dynasty continued its decline into vice and decrepitude. One after the other, the leaders repeated the pattern of incest and murder. The Ptolemies were energetic, intelligent, power-hungry and ruthless. Ptolemy V continued his father's brand of cruelty and indiscriminate use of violence. Having no sister, he was the first of the line who was forced to marry outside the clan. His wife, Cleopatra I, ushered in a new era in the Ptolemy dynasty – that of dynamic and influential women. The women lusted after power and demonstrated their ability to seize and use it as well. This pair reigned until the death of Ptolemy V at the age of 28 whereupon rule was passed to his son, Ptolemy VI. Ptolemy VI later married his sister, Cleopatra II, and they ruled for a time jointly with their brother, Ptolemy VIII until Ptolemy VI was driven out of Egypt and became king of Cyrene. The source of this falling out was undoubtedly the sexual triad the siblings engaged in, which could not be sustained long without an outbreak of jealousies and quarrels.

When Ptolemy VI died in 145 B.C., the monarchy passed to his 16-year-old son by Cleopatra II, Ptolemy VII. Ptolemy VIII did not stand by long and allow his nephew power, however. He married his widowed sister Cleopatra II, and immediately (some say at the wedding itself, in full view of his wife-sister) murdered Ptolemy VII. History has handed down the story that Cleopatra II accepted her brother-husband Ptolemy VIII into her bed that very evening, even though he had so recently killed her son that his hands were still stained with blood! If Cleopatra II had not begun yet to despise Ptolemy VIII, he gave her further reason when he seduced her daughter, Cleopatra III. This pair left Egypt for some time, likely haven been driven out by Cleopatra II, who then ruled alone in their absence. When they returned the three ruled Egypt together for a time, but this could hardly have been a happy alliance. Ptolemy VIII demonstrated a particularly despicable and cruel character. When he perceived his son by Cleopatra II to be a threat at one point, he ordered him killed and dismembered, and delivered the remains to the boy's mother as a "gift". Cleopatra II died, probably having been murdered by her daughter who wished to get her out of the way. Ptolemy VIII and Cleopatra III were married, perhaps even before her mother's death.

Ptolemy VIII died in 116 B.C., leaving Cleopatra III as Queen of Egypt. The most powerful woman yet to come upon the Egyptian scene, Cleopatra III had two sons with her uncle-husband. His will mandated that she rule together with one of them, according to her choice. Cleopatra was partial to her younger son, Ptolemy X, who in his youth was pliable and suggestible and whom

Ptolemy III

she felt she could control. She despised the elder; Ptolemy IX whom she feared was plotting to take over her power and who seemed to have the ability to do so given a chance. Her hatred of her son was quite vehement and she persecuted him with all the fury of her character, which was considerable. Cleopatra's choice was Ptolemy X, although the council of Alexandria strongly apposed her. Ptolemy IX meanwhile took over the government of Cyprus, while his younger brother ruled jointly with their mother. The Alexandrians chafed miserably under Ptolemy X's rule, and wanted his brother to come back. Cleopatra was forced to allow him to return, replacing him in Cyprus with Ptolemy X. IX then ruled with his mother for a time, but she soon hatched a plot to have him exiled by pretending he had been caught plotting her murder. The younger brother then returned from Cyprus and again shared the throne with Cleopatra III. He had gained some maturity during this time however and apparently had grown into some of the Ptolemy greed and lust for power after all. Mother and son had a falling out, and Ptolemy X arranged to have Cleopatra murdered. He took over solo rule, until his death in a naval battle. Ptolemy IX was once more brought back from Cyprus and ruled Egypt until he died at age 62, leaving no legitimate male heir to the throne. Cleopatra Berenice, his daughter and widow of his brother Ptolemy X, ruled for a short time. Egyptian custom forced her to marry her young son Ptolemy XI in order to share power with a male consort. This marriage lasted two and a half weeks, until Ptolemy XI murdered his bride-mother, and was put to death by an angry mob. This inauspicious mess ended the legitimate Ptolemy dynastic line. The year was 80 BC.

Ptolemy IX had, however, produced two sons out of wedlock. These two were given the kingdoms of Egypt and Cyprus. The brother who took the Egyptian crown was Ptolemy XII, known as Auletes, or "the Flute Player", a derogatory moniker bestowed on him by the people who saw him as a weakling and simpleton. We do not know who his mother was, but we know his sister was Cleopatra V, whom he married. Ptolemy Auletes assumed the throne in the year 80 B.C. Preferring to be known as the New Dionysus, he fashioned his image of himself after the god he referred to as his ancestor.

Meanwhile, the great power of the Roman Empire was on the rise, paralleling the demise of the Ptolemaic dynasty. While in Rome political chaos reigned, the Roman armies nevertheless racked up victory after victory abroad. Pompey, Sulla, Crassus and Caesar were

Ptolemy V

leading political figures of the time. Each would take the leading position in his turn, Caesar to be the last.

The Roman leaders increased their interest and control in Egypt during this period. Auletes was not recognized by Rome as the true Egyptian monarch since he did not descend directly along the legitimate Ptolemy line. There were even rumors that the previous Ptolemy Pharaoh had left the kingdom of Egypt to Rome in his will! Since nobody seemed to be able to produce a copy of such a will however, the Romans had to make due with mocking Auletes for being an illegitimate bastard and not deserving of the kingdom. The poor harassed Auletes found himself constantly appeasing Rome through payments of money and treasure, and he lived in perpetual fear that Egypt would at any moment be overrun by Rome, losing its independent status. The Roman senate argued time and again as to what should become of Egypt, with many desiring to make her a Roman province, but in name she remained an ally to Rome for the time being. The Roman leaders exploited Auletes' insecurity and demanded that he deposit monthly sums to the Roman coffers, even though he never received any real promises of legitimacy or help for his situation in return. The people of Egypt accepted his rule, but ridiculed him at the same time, calling him a simple flute-player and deriding his weaknesses.

Ptolemy IX

The Roman Empire meanwhile made inroads into numerous lands of the Mediterranean. When Cyprus was overtaken by Rome, the Alexandrians greatly feared that they would be next in line for such a fate. To become a province of Rome was anathema to the Egyptians, and their patience finally ran out with their weak and ineffectual ruler. When it seemed clear that Auletes would be unable to protect them from the coming threat, he was driven into exile in 59 B.C. and fled to Rome.

Ptolemy X

At this time Rome was a disorganized bed of chaos, and scandals of all kinds infested its political life. Pompey, Crassus, and Caesar received the wealthy foreign visitor with varying degrees of warmth. It was Pompey who went as far as to invite the exiled monarch to live with him as his guest.

The two formed an alliance of sorts, and apparently, a friendship. Pompey stood up to those who tried to convince Rome to reject Ptolemy outright.

Julius Caesar, who had once been the object of Auletes greatest fear, since the former had made an earlier effort to annex Egypt as a province to Rome,

had become a Roman consul. Auletes decided there was no way out save to try to come to some kind of terms with him. Since Caesar was at that time in terrible financial debt, he was amenable to a deal in which Ptolemy Auletes would hand over a one-time payment of a huge sum to Caesar and Pompey, in return for recognition by Rome of his legitimate monarchy in Egypt. Pompey saw a probable political advantage to having the Egyptian king under his wing and Auletes paid enormous sums to uphold his status. He was forced to become involved with unscrupulous moneylenders to keep up with the gigantic payments he promised. As a result of these payments Auletes was returned to his throne in Alexandria, under the protective wing of Pompey who ordered a Roman entourage to accompany the returning king to Alexandria.

A Roman army under Gabinius was dispatched to the East with the King in tow. Gabinius apparently sent a man named Archelaus ahead to Egypt ahead of the army, with the mission of marriage to Ptolemy Auletes' daughter Berenice, who was then ruling in her father's absence.

Once Archelaus had achieved this goal, it became clear what Gabinius' plan had been. Gabinius suddenly declared that he feared Archelaus would lead Egypt in war against Rome! On

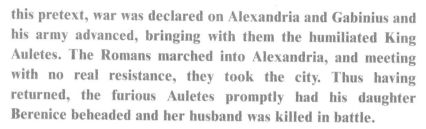

this pretext, war was declared on Alexandria and Gabinius and his army advanced, bringing with them the humiliated King Auletes. The Romans marched into Alexandria, and meeting with no real resistance, they took the city. Thus having returned, the furious Auletes promptly had his daughter Berenice beheaded and her husband was killed in battle.

It was in the midst of the turmoil of her sister's murder, her father's return and Alexandria's takeover by the Romans that the teenaged Cleopatra first laid eyes on Antony. Marc Antony was leading the cavalry charge when the Roman army entered Alexandria. By some accounts Antony was instantly smitten with her charms and impressed by her charisma. This would lead us to believe that even as a very young woman Cleopatra possessed an unusually bewitching way with males. Years would pass and many events would take place before the two would meet again. The murder of her sister had left the fourteen-year-old Cleopatra VII the oldest living offspring of Ptolemy Auletes, and the heir apparent.

• Cleopatra VII •

Cleopatra VII was born in 69 B.C. to Ptolemy Auletes. Her family tree was decorated with powerful rulers, yet stained with crimes of the most abhorrent nature. Her ancestors had engaged in every vice and perversion imaginable, while using their considerable talents and passions, along with cruelty and unrivaled lust for power to maintain the crown for three centuries. History has not recorded the definitive identity of her mother. It has been conjectured that she was Auletes' second wife, whom he married after Cleopatra V had given birth to Berenice IV and Cleopatra VI. Nothing is known about the fate of Cleopatra V, however. She simply disappears from the record. Auletes' sons, Ptolemy XIII and XIV also were apparently born to this unknown wife, and were the full brothers of Cleopatra VII. A younger daughter Arsinoe was also more than likely Cleopatra's full sibling.

Our Cleopatra is said to have possessed a regal appearance and bearing, as well as a passionate and fiery nature and outstanding intellect. From images that have been preserved on coins since antiquity, we surmise that she was not beautiful in the classic sense, her features being pronounced and large. History explains that her physical appeal was considerable however, perhaps due to her hypnotic and piercing gaze, her knowledge of the art of seduction, and her astute use of womanly wiles. Her enormous intelligence combined with her wit and intuitive powers made her stand out as a particularly striking and unusual figure.

Cleopatra was a highly educated young woman. A strong Greek background, including the language and culture of her family's native country had been preserved and handed down the Ptolemy line, although the Ptolemies ruled as Egyptians and were well versed in the culture of their adopted country as well. Cleopatra was multi-lingual, and became the first of the Ptolemy line to undertake to learn the Egyptian language of her subjects. She also studied literature and astronomy, and even dabbled in medicine, science, and mathematics. Her drive and ambition, coupled with her extraordinary mental abilities allowed her to learn and achieve far beyond her peers.

• Alexandria- the Great City •

The city where Cleopatra's ancestors ruled for 3 centuries, and in which she was born and reared was an impressive Mediterranean capital indeed. The city was founded by Alexander the Great, who commissioned its planning and design to the Greek Dinocrates. Alexandria was the first city to be organized with a set of straight streets and paths, running parallel and crossed with one another. Most of these roads were paved and quite wide, which was in great contrast to Rome, where a maze of unpaved narrow and winding alleyways characterized the cityscape.

Arriving in Alexandria from the sea, one would be greeted from a distance of thirty miles by a magnificent lighthouse, which stood on the Island of Pharos, near the harbor. A structure of white marble, the lighthouse stood three stories high and was a design miracle of its age. Indeed the lighthouse of Alexandria was one of the Seven Wonders of the World.

The Royal Palace was a huge structure, which led to the museum and library nearby. Temples built to the many Greek and Egyptian gods and goddesses were plentiful in the city,

including the majestic Temple of Poseidon. The state buildings and government offices were imposing structures, usually surrounded by well-tended gardens with flowering shrubs. The residential buildings had open-air markets on the bottom levels. The Alexandrian library was the largest in the world and a repository for scholarly thought from the entire region. The museum was next to the library, and housed the Alexandrian School. These buildings were arranged in close proximity to the Royal Palace.

Greeks, Egyptians and Jews all lived in the city forming a cacophony of sounds, customs, religions and classes, from very wealthy to pathetically poor.

• Becoming Queen •

Ptolemy XII Auletes ruled as King of Egypt until his death in 51 B.C. The Alexandrians were not resigned to the intense Roman influence of the time, but their king was paying his debts to Rome until the very end. Pompey was named as guardian of the Ptolemy children when their father died. Cleopatra VII was then seventeen years old, and her younger brothers about ten and seven years old respectively. In his will, Ptolemy Auletes bequeathed the throne of Egypt to Cleopatra and her brother Ptolemy XIII. Although Ptolemy was a mere child, Egyptian law and Ptolemy tradition demanded that a female ruler have a consort, so brother and sister were pressed into marriage and supposed co-rule. Cleopatra did her best to negate the boy's power, simply ignoring his existence for the most part, and he might well have remained in the background. He was, however flanked by powerful advisors and who formed a certain following for him among the Alexandrians. Pothinus, a power hungry eunuch, and the powerful statesman, Achillas more than likely understood that Cleopatra was, although young, a force to be reckoned with. They allied themselves with the younger monarch in an effort to make their own inroads into power.

Events in Rome had caused Caesar and Pompey to end their alliance, and Caesar's power was on the rise. The armies of the two great leaders clashed, and Cleopatra, believing Pompey to be the stronger of the two, tried to align herself and Egypt, with him. She sent him naval reinforcements, and shipments of corn for his troops. We can see the beginning of a pattern Cleopatra was to repeat several times over the course of her life and career. She made calculated efforts to align herself in whatever way possible with the current most powerful Roman leader, as she saw this as the way to ensure her own continuing power. When Pompey's son Cneius came to Egypt with a request for help for his father, the Queen saw this as an opportunity to link her own rise with that of the Roman leader, and was more than glad to oblige.

Meanwhile, Pothinus and Achillas and their followers in Alexandria helped Ptolemy XIII instigate revolt in Egypt in an effort to overthrow his sister's rule. It is likely that public opinion had been turned against Cleopatra on the charge that she was assisting the Romans. When Ptolemy VIII turned 14 years old he was given a formal coronation. His supporters no doubt used this occasion to whip up emotional support for the young monarch, and to downplay the Queen. The civil conflict that ensued was driven by a desire by the young king and his party to do away with Cleopatra. Given what we know about the Ptolemy ruthlessness and the propensity for sibling and spousal murder, can we have any doubt that this was the goal? However, Cleopatra, along with her sister Arsinoe, managed to escape and flee to Syria.

The advisors stepped into the void, taking over Ptolemy's council of regency, and ruled Egypt using the child king as a puppet.

Caesar defeated Pompey in the great confrontation at Pharsalus. After this decisive battle, Caesar was seen as the undisputed leader of the Roman Empire. The broken

Pompey was adrift with his navy in the Mediterranean, searching for help and refuge. Since he was officially the guardian of Ptolemy XIII and had provided help to the young king's father in the past, he naturally considered Egypt a possible friend and ally. He set his sails toward Alexandria in hopes of finding asylum there.

It was not to be. Ptolemy XIII was notified of Pompey's approach, and as the ships made their way to Egypt, the king's advisors conferred as to the most strategic response. History offers several explanations for their decision, including fear that Pompey would try to invade Egypt. A more plausible reason perhaps was the thought that a dead Pompey would be feather in Egypt's cap in the eyes of Caesar, who now held all the power. At any rate, the order was given to trap Pompey by luring him to shore with promises. The Egyptians then murdered him in cold blood in full view of his fleet. The fifteen-year-old Ptolemy XIII observed the killing from his perch on shore. The boy had begun to show his true Ptolemy colors and emerged as a crafty and dangerous character in his own right.

Caesar was also traveling the Mediterranean waters following the battle of Pharsalus, and arrived in Alexandria with his legions several days later. It is sometimes said that Caesar came to Egypt because he desired to meet Cleopatra whose charms had somehow become known to him by way of rumor. It is far more likely however, that Caesar simply pursued Pompey as he fled following the battle of Pharsalus, not wanting him to be able to hide in Egypt, and wanting to claim Egypt for himself and the Roman Empire which he himself now controlled. The year was 48 B.C.

Cleopatra (to Alexas):
See where he is, who's with him, what he does:
I did not send you. If you find him sad,[1]
Say I am dancing; if in mirth, report
That I am sudden sick.

1.Serious

**From Shakespeare: Antony and Cleopatra
Act 1, scene 3**

Caesar arrived knowing nothing of the fate that had befallen Pompey. As he came ashore the Alexandrians greeted him and presented him with Pompey's head. The shocked leader did not regale them with congratulations, but instead bowed in mourning for his onetime friend and erstwhile foe.

After making sure that Pompey received a proper burial, Caesar strode regally into Alexandria and took up residence at the royal palace. The Egypt Caesar found was torn between

their two sibling leaders. King Ptolemy XIII was at that time in Pelusium with his army making ready to counter any attempt by Cleopatra to retake the crown. Ptolemy XIII was apparently terrified to confront the Caesar, and for the time being stayed with his armies rather than return to his own palace. Caesar sent communications to both of the estranged monarchs suggesting reconciliation. He saw no reason to favor one over the other at that point, so his sentiments were probably neutral and driven by a wish to take over Egypt for Rome efficiently and quickly without a battle.

Cleopatra had not been idle during her exile. She had immediately gone into action aimed at returning to Egypt to oust her brother and his retinue and to retake the throne. Though as yet only a young woman of 21, she succeeded in raising an army in Syria and amassed it to the east of Egypt. Now that Caesar was the leader of the Roman Empire rather than Pompey, and especially since Caesar was now residing in the royal palace in Alexandria, Cleopatra realized that her next move was not to attack her brother's forces, but to go directly

to the top with her bid for favor by Rome. Things seemed at a stalemate as Caesar resided comfortably in the palace and continued to behave as if Rome had already taken over Egypt. The young Ptolemy's advisors grew nervous, and Pothinus brought the king back to Alexandria, leaving Achillas near Pelusium with the army. Still unwilling to confront Caesar, the boy king lived as a sort of guest of the Roman in his own palace. His hatred and fear of Caesar were well hidden behind feigned friendly and polite behavior. We can presume that the king and his advisors were lying in wait, wondering how to get the better of the Roman. Caesar, lacking a

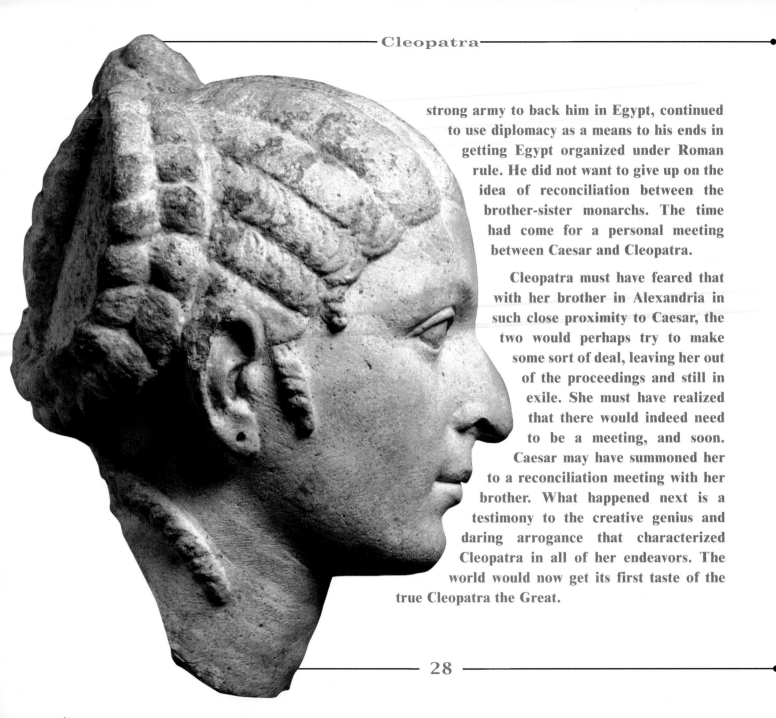

strong army to back him in Egypt, continued to use diplomacy as a means to his ends in getting Egypt organized under Roman rule. He did not want to give up on the idea of reconciliation between the brother-sister monarchs. The time had come for a personal meeting between Caesar and Cleopatra.

Cleopatra must have feared that with her brother in Alexandria in such close proximity to Caesar, the two would perhaps try to make some sort of deal, leaving her out of the proceedings and still in exile. She must have realized that there would indeed need to be a meeting, and soon. Caesar may have summoned her to a reconciliation meeting with her brother. What happened next is a testimony to the creative genius and daring arrogance that characterized Cleopatra in all of her endeavors. The world would now get its first taste of the true Cleopatra the Great.

• Meeting Caesar •

The Queen desired more than anything the return to her place on the throne of Egypt. Her plot was hatched with this single goal uppermost in mind. She realized the Caesar was her only hope and aimed her actions at attaining his favor. She bargained all on the knowledge that she must preempt her brother in a dramatic fashion to gain Caesar's attention. One wonders if Cleopatra would have gained any notoriety at all in the pages of history had Caesar not appeared in Alexandria at precisely this juncture. Perhaps her fate would have been similar to those of the previous female Ptolemy rulers. The fact that the great Roman was there for the influencing opened up a great opportunity for Cleopatra, and she certainly did not waste it.

When Caesar arrived in Alexandria he was preceded by his reputation not just as a warrior and conqueror, but also as a lover of women with a string of amorous adventures to his name. Caesar considered himself of godly descent, and claimed Venus, the god of love, as his ancestor. A married man in his fifties, plagued by a receding hairline, Caesar left his third wife waiting for him in Rome while he garnered the nickname "the bald adulterer". Cleopatra probably bargained on his being susceptible to calculated use of her considerable womanly gifts.

Cleopatra employed only one servant, Appolodorus, to help her with her plan.

The two boarded a small craft, and sailed from Pelusium to Alexandria at dusk. As they approached their destination Cleopatra might have pondered the fact that she was in fact risking her future on the success of the escapade. How confident of her own charms and of the man's vulnerabilities she must have been. Was she terrified? Or was she quite certain that success would be had. As the twenty-one year old Queen and her servant slipped into the bay at Alexandria, did

Cleopatra quiver with excitement and anticipation, or did she experience sudden regrets at the capriciousness of her plan?

As darkness fell, the little boat gained the harbor, and Appolodorus rowed it to the dock near the royal palace. Using a carpet, or perhaps sheets of bedding, her helper rolled Cleopatra into a bundle, which they hoped looked like something being delivered to the palace. Tying the package with rope, he slung it over his shoulder, and walked up to the palace, causing the spies Pothinus had posted not so much as a raised eyebrow. Requesting permission to deliver his goods directly to Caesar, Appolodorus was shown into the chambers of the Roman, and there he lowered his burden to the floor. He untied the knots, and all at once, Cleopatra sprang to her feet in front of Caesar!

Julius Caesar

Just as Cleopatra had bargained for, the great leader was delightfully surprised and impressed with the amazing young woman who had dared to contrive such a feat! He had desired to meet her, and assumed she would arrive presently, but never had he imagined such an entrance, and at her own initiative. Perhaps due to his own sense of adventure or his natural appreciation for a prank well executed, he regarded the woman who stood before him as obviously special and fascinating. When Cleopatra began to speak with her melodious voice, and fixed her intense gaze on his, Caesar was spellbound and charmed in every way possible.

Did Caesar perhaps see before him for the first time in his glorious career, a woman who was his counterpart in every sense? Her intellect

Cleopatra was laid on a bed without any finery or glory. When Caesar entered the room, she suddenly got up in only her smock, and fell at his feet – disfigured. She had ripped hair from her head and had raked her face with her nails. Her voice was small and trembling and she blubbered continually, her eyes were sunken in her head, and most of her stomach had been ripped at. In short, her body was not much better than her mind, yet her good grace and the force of her beauty had not been altogether erased.

From Plutarch
"Life of Marcus Antonius" in The Lives of the Noble Grecians and Romans

matched his own, her wit and genius were impressive. Did he feel himself in the presence of greatness? While we have said that Cleopatra was perhaps not a raving beauty in the usual sense, we can't deny that her physical attractiveness and magnetism were substantial. Caesar apparently saw no reason to prolong their meeting into a courtship, and the two became lovers that very evening. The mighty Julius Caesar had met a woman he could not resist, and who seemed to rival him in raw power and charisma. They immediately became inseparable and all who witnessed the pair were taken with the intoxicated way they were drawn to one another.

The morning that followed Caesar and Cleopatra's first night of love dawned on a different Egypt, although none could have been aware of it so soon. The events in Caesar's bedroom had caused the tide to turn in Alexandria, and although Caesar was still bent on facilitating reconciliation between his lover and her husband-brother, his affection for Cleopatra would seal all of their fates in ways he could not yet foresee.

When the young King Ptolemy was summoned to the Romans' chamber and his eyes fell on his sister, he immediately understood what had transpired and grasping that she had achieved a great coup and its significance for his position, he was filled with a murderous Ptolemy wrath. The king ran outside screaming his betrayal by Cleopatra and gathered supporters to riot and storm the palace.

Caesar managed to appease the crowd, and called a meeting where he read out the will of Auletes, which had called for co-rule of Ptolemy XIII and Cleopatra VII. He claimed he was trying to uphold the spirit of their

---

Caesar:
Bravest at the last,
She leveled at[1] our purposes, and
    being royal,
Took her own way…

…She hath pursued conclusions[2]
    infinite
Of easy ways to die. Take up her
    bed,
And bear her women from the
    monument.
She shall be buried by her Antony.
No grave upon the earth shall clip[3]
    in it
A pair so famous. High events as
    these
Strike[4] those that make them; and
    their story is
No less in pity, than his glory which
Brought them to be lamented…

1. i. Guessed ii. Fought against
2. experiments
3. clasp
4. touch

**From Shakespeare: Antony and Cleopatra
Act V, scene 2**

previous king's wishes in attempting to reconcile the two. Caesar, as leader of the Roman Empire ordered that the pair be prevailed upon to agree to resume their co-rule of Egypt. They did so, though it seems clear that underneath their official behavior, an intense hatred for one another festered.

The reconciliation was hailed with great celebration and feasting in Alexandria. The festival was of such a grand scale that the even the great Roman general, used to every luxury, must have marveled at its opulence and magnificence. The party was held in a room, which resembled a glorious temple, the walls paneled with pure ivory and the pillars covered in shimmering gold. Hundreds of slaves served the merry-makers and the food was a vast selection of succulent and unusual dishes. The tables and cutlery were of ivory and gold, and most excellent wines flowed freely. The heads of the guests were adorned with crowns of fragrant roses.

Queen Cleopatra was dressed in a shimmering gown made of a filmy transparent fabric. Her limbs and neck were strung with priceless precious jewels. She was served while lying on a couch next to her husband-brother Ptolemy, while Caesar lay close by.

After the food and wine were cleared away, Caesar rose to speak to the assembled celebrants. He professed a deep curiosity about the land of Egypt, announcing his desire to travel extensively in country, to learn the language, and to study the inscriptions on the temples and monuments in order to learn about the origins and past of the people. The epitome of his curiosity was directed at finding what had previously eluded all who had searched for it – the secret source of the Nile River.

• The Alexandrian War •

Caesar could certainly have gone back to Rome after accomplishing the reconciliation of the king and Queen, and it probably would have been appropriate for him to do so, leaving the Egyptians to their own devices. His presence angered the Alexandrians who were absolutely not enamored of so much Roman interference, and the knowledge that their Queen was now the mistress of a Roman general was not at all well received. Caesar and Cleopatra made no effort to conceal their affair, and their love was obviously growing in intensity as time passed. This unashamed betrayal of her spouse-brother was cause for criticism among the Egyptian people who worshipped both of their monarchs as gods, as they had all the previous Ptolemaic rulers. But Caesar stayed on in Alexandria, unable to tear himself away from his passionate affair with the Queen. Cleopatra basked in the support of the dictator for her throne, while lavishing him with every pleasure of the flesh and senses.

Pothinus was furious that all of his efforts to get rid of Cleopatra had come to naught and incensed that she was now cavorting in the palace with the Roman ruler. Since the young King Ptolemy was now reduced to a secondary appendage that answered to Caesar, Pothinus felt his own power ebbing away. Pothinus was now supposedly a member of Caesar's camp, since he was advisor to the king, who had officially reconciled with the Queen. The three supposedly occupied the palace in harmony. Beneath this charade however, a hatred of Caesar and Cleopatra burned in the eunuch's breast, and he contrived to stir things up again. He still had control of the armies of Ptolemy XIII who were waiting in Pelusium under the command of Achillas, and he called them to Alexandria. When their actual commander, Ptolemy XIII sent a message, through

Caesar, for them to halt their advance, Achillas simply ignored this directive and proceeded toward the city. About fourteen days after the celebration festival, war was declared and the Egyptian army attacked with the aim of driving the Queen and her Roman protector out.

Caesar had come to Alexandria with only a small force, and the Roman troops had to fight fiercely against an Egyptian army six times the size of their own. It would be no simple matter to put down this threat. The entire Alexandrian population rose against Caesar along with the army of Achillas. The battle raged within the confines of the city and along the harbor.

In the early days of the war, Arsinoe, sister of the king and Queen, escaped the house arrest in the palace, which she and her brother the king had been placed under by Caesar, and defected to Achillas and the Alexandrians. The Alexandrians haled her as their new Queen. Cleopatra would later show how resentful and angry she had been at the act of betrayal by her sister. Arsinoe ordered Achillas' murder when quarrels broke out between her faithful eunuch Ganymedes and the general. She then appointed Ganymedes commander of the Egyptian forces.

Meanwhile in the palace, Caesar had Pothinus executed, thereby doing away with the enemy that had lurked within his own walls. One wonders what took Caesar so long to discover that Pothinus was in cahoots with Achillas from the outset. Caesar also allowed young Ptolemy XIII his liberty when the youngster declared he wanted to go the Alexandrians for a meeting to negotiate peace. He apparently wanted to cleanse the palace of all who represented opposition, and to get rid of his mistress's husband. Caesar said a solemn good-bye to Ptolemy as the youngster set out to join the enemy. Accounts of the scene report that the boy cried with grief at his leave-taking and declared his undying friendship to the Roman. Caesar however was not taken in, and in the end he summarily dismissed him. As was to be expected, the moment the boy was released he joined the fight against the Cleopatra and the Romans with all of his heart and energy. He became the leader of the Egyptian army, the fate of Ganymedes being unclear.

As the war raged, the Alexandrians took control of the island of Pharos, and fearing they would use that position to take over his naval vessels, Caesar set fire to them, and to the entire Egyptian fleet. The huge fire raged for days, crossing the harbor and setting alight many of the glorious buildings of Alexandria. Perhaps the greatest tragedy of the Alexandrian war was the loss of the Great Library. The contents of the library were almost entirely burned, destroying forever the record of Greek and Roman civilization that had been contained within its walls. The museum that stood alongside the library was also destroyed.

Caesar made a desperate attempt to overtake the island of Pharos, and was able to recover it and the Heptastadium. He succeeded, but the buildings on the island were destroyed in this battle. When the Egyptians tried to overtake the Heptastadium, Caesar was forced to jump into the water and swim for safety.

Finally, in March 47 B.C., reinforcements from Rome arrived to shore up Caesar's depleted legions. The army of Mithradates together with Caesar's forces which had until now been defending one quarter of the city, surprised Ptolemy's forces in the dead of night, and annihilated them. King Ptolemy XIII tried to escape up the Nile, but his vessel capsized and he met a watery death. His gold suit of armor was retrieved for Caesar and sent to Alexandria as proof of his demise. The war had lasted six months.

• Caesar and Cleopatra •

Caesar returned to Alexandria as the triumphant victor. The Alexandrians awaited his arrival with quaking fear as to their fate. In mourning garments they greeted the Roman troops as they marched back into the damaged and war-torn city. Caesar greatly surprised them by greeting the people warmly. Applying no punishment whatever on the citizens he instead ordered them to rebuild their once magnificent city and to restore it to its former glory.

Caesar had no wish to hand over a grieving populace to his mistress' rule. He wanted her capital to thrive once more and to be a tribute again to Alexander the Great. For all his ability to fight fiercely and even cruelly when necessary, Caesar was a compassionate man, who especially compared with the norms of his time, behaved in a particularly humane manner.

Since there is no record of Cleopatra's activities during the Alexandrian war, we have to be content to conjecture that she was for the time at least, the woman behind the man, at home in the royal palace, providing comfort and pleasure, and perhaps advice, to the great Caesar.

When the war ended, Caesar handed the rule of Egypt to his lover and her younger brother, Ptolemy XIV, who was then only a child of eleven. Their father, Ptolemy XII had specified in his will that Cleopatra must rule along with one of her brothers, and the demise of Ptolemy XIII made it the turn of the even younger sibling. Since the Egyptian custom was that sibling co-rulers should marry, Cleopatra became the wife of Ptolemy XIV. Caesar made sure that the boy was strictly watched and supervised so as not to become a threat in any way, and Cleopatra was the actual and undisputed monarch. As for their treacherous sister, Arsinoe, Caesar had her exiled and she spent the next few years in Rome.

With the war over and Cleopatra restored to sole rule of Egypt, Caesar was free to return to Rome or at least to occupy himself with its politics and events concerning his empire. Certainly the Romans assumed he would return at any moment, as things in Rome were chaotic and unsettled, and much had occurred while the dictator had been detained in Egypt. Yet, he remained. There can be little doubt that the great leader was in love with Cleopatra, and that his time spent in Egypt was for the most part in order to be near her. Even his great curiosity and thirst for knowledge of Egyptian history and the source of the Nile would undoubtedly have played second fiddle to his need to keep the Roman politics in hand, had he not enjoyed such a satisfactory life with the Queen of Egypt.

Enobarbus:
The barge she sat in, like a
    burnished throne,
Burned on the water: the poop was
    beaten gold;
Purple the sails, and so perfumed that
The winds were lovesick with them;
    the oars were silver,
Which to the tune of flutes kept
    stroke and made
The water which they beat to follow
    faster,
As amorous of their strokes. For her
    own person,
It beggared all description: she did lie
In her pavilion, cloth-of-gold of
    tissue,[1]
O'erpicturing that Venus where we
    see
The fancy outwork nature:[2] on each
    side her
Stood pretty dimpled boys, like
    smiling Cupids,
With divers-colored fans, whose wind
    did seem
To glow the delicate cheeks which
    they did cool,
And what they undid did.[3]
...From the barge
A strange invisible perfume hits the
    sense
Of the adjacent wharfs[4]...

...I saw her once
Hop forty paces through the public
  street;
And having lost her breath, she
  spoke, and panted,
That[5] she did make defect
  perfection,
And, breathless, pow'r breathe forth.

... Age cannot wither her, nor
  custom stale
Her infinite variety: other women
  cloy
The appetites they feed, but she
makes hungry
Where most she satisfies; for vilest
  things

Among the Alexandrians there was considerable consternation around the continuing presence of Caesar in their midst, and his relationship with their Queen irked them all the more. That an Egyptian Queen should enter into such a liaison with a Roman general was shocking and unprecedented. Cleopatra and Caesar made no attempts to hide their affair from the populace, and when presently the Queen became pregnant there was hardly a question as to whose child she carried. Since she was married, however, to Ptolemy XIV, he would be the legitimate father of the child, a consequence unacceptable to all concerned. To solve this problem, Cleopatra enlisted the help of priests. The holy men declared that Caesar was actually an embodiment of the god Ammon, and that the deity was the true father of the expected child! The Egyptian religion recognized such phenomena, and it was accepted without question that a god could create a royal child with a sovereign. This put to rest all questions of impropriety concerning Cleopatra's

Become themselves[6] in her, that the holy priests
Bless her when she is riggish.[7]

1. a rich fabric interwoven with gold threads
2. surpassing that painting of Venus where we can see the imagination excelling nature itself in creative ability
3. and seemed to produce the warm color they were cooling
4. banks
5. so that
6. are becoming
7. wanton

From Shakespeare: Antony and Cleopatra Act 11, scene 2

pregnancy. Caesar was likely thrilled with the prospect of perhaps being presented with the male offspring that none of his wives had as yet been able to produce.

As time went on and Caesar still did not return to Rome it must have become quiet apparent that this was no simple matter of a mistress pleasing a powerful man with her sexual favors. Caesar never tired of Cleopatra's company and consulted her in matters of state and politics, knowing that her sharp intellect and intuition would never fail to provide good counsel. They discussed every subject deeply and intelligently, each fascinated by what the other had to say. Even in military matters Cleopatra had a wide ranging understanding of strategy, and although history leaves no record of such, we must surmise that she was with him behind the scenes during the Alexandrian war, suggesting, though probably not directing Caesar's moves. Cleopatra's wide-ranging education made her an able partner in discourse with Caesar. Like him, she had an active curious mind, never ceasing to attain more and more knowledge.

This is not to say of course that activities in the bedroom were not extremely satisfying to Caesar. The Queen was well versed in the sensual arts and could demonstrate a feminine softness and vulnerability as well as a determined hardness of spirit. Cleopatra was slim and probably tall, and her hair was jet black and abundant. Her movements were graceful, but demonstrated a certain amount of haughtiness. Her charm was bewitching to men, and Caesar had certainly fallen under her womanly spell. He was fascinated and delighted by her many contrasts. She was a contemplative planner when called for, and patiently plotted before acting. Yet she could be exciting and stimulating, and sometimes showed a spontaneous fury and passion. Caesar was certainly never bored in her presence, whether by day, or by night.

● A Royal Cruise ●

Caesar had apparently not been spouting empty words when he purported to be fascinated with Egyptian culture and desirous of learning more about his mistress's land. Together with Cleopatra, he set off on a Nile River journey to study the art, religions, and landscapes of the country. The pair took to the river with a fleet of four hundred craft, led by their official vessel of state which was outfitted with every luxury and lavishly equipped to ensure the comfort of its important passengers. This boat was fifty feet high and reached a height of several stories, each surrounded by balconies and decks. Its rooms and apartments were large and splendidly furnished. Semi-precious stones were used to adorn and decorate the pillars and colonnades.

Caesar and Cleopatra sailed the Nile past many cities, visiting shrines and sites, giving Caesar every opportunity to become acquainted with the Egypt that existed beyond the walls of the capital. Along their route they observed the site of the Great Pyramids, a thrill for the Roman leader and Cleopatra alike. After six or seven weeks the vessels returned home to Alexandria, Caesar now knowing far more about Egypt and the lovers having enjoyed a pleasant and interesting journey.

• Caesar Departs Egypt •

The Alexandrian war was several months in the past, Cleopatra was securely on her throne, and the Nile journey had been completed. Caesar must have felt he could delay his departure from Egypt no longer. Matters in Rome had become alarming, following a defeat in Asia Minor, and needed his attention at once. He left Alexandria in early June, only weeks before the birth of Cleopatra's child – his son, whom she named Caesarion. Caesar received word of his son's birth while fighting a short battle in Asia Minor from which he emerged the victor. Cleopatra rejoiced at home at the birth of her son, and ordered that coins be minted with her image holding her newborn.

Caesar returned to Rome to attend to the business of the empire. We can assume he resumed his life with his faithful and patient wife, Calpurnia. Over the next two years he participated in several more military adventures, until September 45 B.C. when he returned for the last time to Rome. Caesar worked tirelessly to reorganize the government and to solve the more pressing problems of Roman society, where the people were demoralized by unemployment, debts, and anarchy. As part of his plan to remodel the entire city of Rome, Caesar commissioned plans for a great library to be built. It was to be modeled after the Alexandrian library, which had been lost in the great conflagration he had caused during the war. He also laid out plans for temples and buildings of all kinds, as well as a canal connecting the Anio and Tiber rivers, and a dam to keep the sea back from eroding the outskirts of the city. This reconstruction of Rome did not take place during Caesar's lifetime, but it was he who had the vision and commissioned the original design.

Cleopatra's beauty was not the kind that surpassed that of other women, nor did it immediately capture the hearts of men, but her company and conversation was so "sweet" that men were immediately taken with her. Her beauty, her good grace, her conversation, and her courteous nature reached man's core. Furthermore, her voice and words were magical, as her tongue was an instrument of music and she could easily talk any language she pleased.

From Plutarch
"Life of Marcus Antonius" in The Lives of the Noble Grecians and Romans

In late 46 B.C. Cleopatra and the infant Caesarion made their way to Rome to be reunited with Caesar. Her brother-husband, the now thirteen-year-old King Ptolemy XIV accompanied them for the sake of propriety and to assure no powerful advisors in Egypt would exert undue influence upon him in the Queen's absence. It is not known for certain whether Cleopatra decided unilaterally to make the trip, or if Caesar invited her. Cleopatra may have worried that 'out of sight – out of mind' and felt that physical proximity to her lover was necessary to insure Caesar's continuing support for her rule of Egypt.

Invited or not, Cleopatra waited until Caesar had been gone half a year, and appeared in Rome only after his various military triumphs had been celebrated. It was during one of these triumphal parades that Cleopatra's sister Arsinoe, a prisoner of Rome, was led through the streets in chains, and the Romans would have seen it as the height of vulgarity for the Queen to be present to her own sister's humiliation. The Roman populace pitied Arsinoe and could not have known how much Cleopatra despised her sister and wished only for her to be executed!

We can only imagine with what pomp and pageantry the Queen Cleopatra was welcomed to Rome. While she hailed from a country already under Roman rule, she would have been hailed as befitted the Queen of a friendly land. Calpurnia, Caesar's wife, had to look on as the official welcoming ceremonies and celebrations took place. As for Caesar, he quickly resumed his affair with Cleopatra, visiting her and his son regularly in the household he had set up for them in an outlying neighborhood of Rome.

Cleopatra lived a relatively quiet life while in Rome. Uncharacteristically, she spoke little and behaved demurely, endeavoring to maintain a low profile so as not to stir more scandal than was necessary. In addition to her lover, she received men of state and others who came to pay their respects to the visiting monarch. It is even likely that Marc Antony, whom Caesar promoted to Consul, was a visitor to her estate, and that the two had an opportunity to renew their acquaintance at this time. They may have discussed their first meeting, when as a teenager Cleopatra witnessed her father returning to Alexandria under the protection of Antony and his cavalry troops.

Cleopatra's presence in Rome was not politically advantageous to Caesar. Public opinion was outraged at the idea that their leader would bring an Egyptian Queen to reside in their midst, just as the Alexandrians had disapproved of the Roman in their city! The facts that the Queen had her own husband residing with her and that Caesar had a wife, only served to fuel their disgust. Roman society was not fond of Egyptians in general and this Queen in particular, and looked down upon her with hostility. That she was in fact of Greek descent was not taken in to account in Rome, as for centuries the Ptolemaic rulers had taken on Egyptian habits and by Cleopatra's time had absorbed Egyptian identity. Cleopatra's behavior was not as a one subservient to Rome, even though her country had already fallen under Roman rule, and she behaved as an equal to the great politicians of Rome, inspiring hate and even fear among them.

Some have conjectured that Caesar's relationship with her was motivated not by love and attraction but by the wish to be associated with an actual descendent of Alexander the Great, and that his motivations at continuing the liaison were only political. But there should be no doubt that theirs was a true affair of the heart, at least on the side of Caesar, and one which he was unwilling to shed, even given the reactions in Rome to his behavior. That Caesar had sincere affection for Cleopatra is given evidence by the fact that he ordered the dedication of a gold bust of the Queen, which was erected in the Temple of Venus, where it was paid divine honors. According the customs of the age, this was an expression of more than admiration between heads of state, or even between ordinary lovers.

Caesar definitely had feelings for Cleopatra, but it might be an exaggeration to say that she inspired him and that his conquests and political moves were somehow connected to her influence. Caesar possessed his own outstanding creative genius and ambition, and his schemes and plans were undoubtedly none but his own. Some have charged that his weakness for Cleopatra caused him to let down his guard and make some wrong moves which ultimately led to his demise. It is quite possible that during his visits to his mistress Caesar discussed matters of state with her and sought her council as he had done in Alexandria. However, as strong as Cleopatra's hold may have been on the man, it is generally agreed that Caesar made his political decisions guided by his courage, vision, and clear independent mind. The Queen may have been his intellectual equal, but she was after all a comparatively inexperienced woman, at least 30 years his junior.

It is of some curiosity, given the affection Caesar obviously felt for Cleopatra, that he did not find it fitting to declare his son by her legal heir to Rome. He in fact had a will drawn up during the period that Cleopatra and Caesarion resided in Rome, in which there was no mention of the child. It is likely he still hoped that his wife would provide him with a male baby in time, yet the deliberate omission of Caesarion stands out. The will named Caesar's nephew Octavian as successor, by way of posthumous adoption, should no legal heir be born in the meantime. We don't know whether Cleopatra was aware at this time of the will being drawn or of its contents concerning the appointed heir to the empire.

While Caesar continued his conquests and his power grew ever greater, Cleopatra quietly and privately wielded her influence, no doubt planning soon to turn her link to the great man to her advantage as events unfolded. We will never know what her secret ambitions were, or what she envisioned for the future. Did she plan somehow to become Caesar's wife, eventually presiding with him side by side over the great Roman Empire? Or did she content herself with keeping the throne of Egypt, wishing only to maintain its security by her continuing affair with the man who held the power of Rome and would champion her cause? After all, her lover had been named Imperator, and Dictator for Life, and was the most powerful man Rome had ever known. Since it was not her nature to exist as a retiring mistress for very long, we must assume that great ideas gestated in her breast, waiting for the proper moment for fruition. Surely she saw no reason to assume that Caesar would not remain dictator of Rome for the better part of her lifetime, with the possibilities for her own career then being limitless. Cleopatra never did anything, nor behaved in any manner, which was not steeped in forethought and purpose, or which was not calculated to support her ambitions. Cleopatra no doubt rejoiced in the fact that her lover was becoming ever more powerful and bided her time until she could turn this to her own advantage.

• The Murder of Julius Caesar •

During the last years of the great dictator's life, there were many seeming contradictions. Some believed he desired nothing more than to crown himself King, but several times rejected coronation. Antony, Caesar's staunch supporter, presented Caesar with a crown on three separate occasions and begged him to become monarch. Caesar declined the coronation, and told him "Jupiter alone is king". While his enemies feared he was becoming too powerful, there were also those who pointed to his refusal of the crown as an indication of righteousness. He was heard to utter that he was tiring of life and had already had enough triumph and glory for one man. Was he becoming apathetic and losing his desire to live on and accomplish more? Caesar suffered at times from epileptic fits, and these perhaps became worse and more frequent with advancing age, increasing his pessimistic and fatalistic attitudes of mind. He took no special measures at personal protection, behaving in a sort of "come what may" manner. . He maintained his regal pride until the very end, and expected deference from every quarter, insisting that his word be treated as law. Yet his attention was concentrated fully on his own plans and schemes, and he paid little attention to those around him.

In February of 44 B.C. Caesar returned to Rome after a stunning defeat of the sons of his deceased enemy Pompey. Caesar was expected to address the Senate on March 15th, after which he was to set out again immediately to a battle on foreign soil. On March 14th Caesar reported strange dreams, in one of which he reached out his hand to Jupiter. That same night his wife dreamed that Caesar lay dead in her arms. The next morning he felt poorly and debated the wisdom of attending the Senate, where the assembly already awaited his arrival. Calpurnia

begged him not to go, and even his doctors advised rest. He was reminded that a soothsayer had recently warned him that he would find death on the Ides of March. But Caesar, who believed in fate and only hoped that when he did find death it would be sudden, refused to have his guard up and did not see what was coming. After hearing the objections of his wife and advisors, he discarded them, and ignoring his own intuitions and misgivings, he made his way to the Senate.

For weeks beforehand, a conspiracy to do away with Caesar had been brewing. Cassius and Brutus, due to their worry that the dictator was becoming too much of a threat, conceived and perfected, along with a group of other senators, a plan to assassinate him. Brutus, the leader of the conspirators, was a man Caesar trusted and respected, and would never have suspected would carry out such a deed against him.

The deliberations as to the whether he might stay at home that day had made him late, and when Caesar entered the Senate floor, all were already assembled. The unsuspecting senators all rose and the conspirators moved forward removing concealed daggers from their cloaks. One by one they fell on him repeatedly stabbed him all over his body. The first few blows were not fatal, and Caesar tried to defend himself against his attackers. When he saw that Brutus too was coming toward him with his dagger drawn, Caesar ceased to resist, and covering his face with his robes, he succumbed to his fate. The assassins' strikes were so numerous and wild that they themselves suffered injuries in the scuffle. As shocked senators looked on silently, the great imperator slumped dead against a statue of Pompey, covering it with blood.

Antony, who had tarried outside the senate, upon hearing about the horrific acts which had taken place inside, removed his official consul garments and quickly disguised himself as a slave. Antony was at that time the most powerful man in Rome next to Caesar, and he had reason to fear for his own life. In fact, the conspirators had previously discussed murdering Antony as well, but had decided against it, a decision they may have later regretted. Antony quickly escaped the senate compound and ran through the streets of Rome as the news of Caesar's death echoed through the city and beyond. Antony managed to reach his home undetected, and barricaded himself within. By sending his son as messenger, he contacted Calpurnia, Caesar's wife, who her grief was suggestible to whatever Antony proposed. She handed over Caesar's fortune and documents to him for safekeeping. Thus Antony succeeded in keeping administrative matters under his control.

The day after the assassination, Brutus and Cassius addressed the public at the forum. Proclaiming tyranny dead and freedom restored they expected jubilant ovations, but their speeches did not ignite the people's passions. Instead, Lepidus, who supposedly supported Antony and the pro-Caesar camp, succeeded in convincing the crowd that Caesar's death was a horrible crime, which must be avenged! Lepidus probably wanted to seize power for himself, but Antony was in no position to reject his purported alliance.

Brutus

When Caesar's will was read and the people of Rome realized that the Imperator had left each citizen a respectable sum, and that he'd appointed Decimus Brutus (one of the senators that had murdered him in cold blood) as guardian of any child that might be born to him, many were moved by the irony and tragedy of the situation. By the time the funeral took place, there was genuine mourning for him among the people, and the conspirators were condemned and criticized.

On the day of the funeral, Caesar's body was shrouded in purple and carried to a pyre upon a white gurney. Antony rose, stood before the corpse and faced the crowd.

While not a great orator by any means, Antony did not on this occasion require outstanding speaking skill to stir the emotions of those present. He recounted the career of Caesar, his numerous and glorious victories for Rome, as well as his generosity and humanity toward the people. After extolling the virtues of the dead leader, Antony's funeral oration continued with an attack on Brutus and Cassius, and he managed to incite public opinion soundly against them. He brandished Caesar's bloodstained robes and shouted that those responsible were murderers and villains. A mob of citizens stormed the homes of the conspirators, and in a frenzy fueled by anger and grief, killed an innocent man who was in fact a supporter of Caesar and Antony!

Caesar's body was set alight and the fire was kept burning for hours as the mourners heaped more fuel upon the pyre. Antony looked on with satisfaction at the sorrow of the people. He assumed the conspirators would now depart Rome in fear and shame, opening the way for him to take over where Caesar had left off. When this did not happen right away, in the succeeding days Antony had to face them all in the senate. He was forced to change his tune slightly and began to speak scornfully of Caesar, purporting to disdain the idea of dictatorship and passing a law in the senate banning future leaders from taking so much power. He had not, however, abandoned his plan to become heir to Caesar and to take over the rule of the empire.

While all of this took place, Caesar's nineteen-year-old nephew Octavian had been away from Rome, waiting with his armies for his uncle to join him. When he received the news of what had happened, more than a week had already passed since Caesar's death. Octavian immediately began to behave as though Caesar had not only posthumously adopted him and made him heir to his possessions, but as if he had also been bequeathed the Roman Empire and it's rule. He determined to behave as Caesar's son in every regard, and to step up and take over power. Octavian began to move his army toward Rome, ready to engage Antony and his forces in civil war over ultimate control.

• Cleopatra Leaves Rome •

There is no record of Cleopatra's whereabouts or movements on the day of Caesar's murder, or during its immediate aftermath. We don't know if she was present at his funeral or if she heard Antony's impassioned eulogy. We can only conjecture that her shock and grief upon hearing of Caesar's demise must have been intense and real. Perhaps she did not grieve Caesar with the pure sense of loss that his wife Calpurnia felt, but she assuredly felt the acute loss of her ally and powerful protector. After the first waves of confusion Cleopatra probably felt fear, for herself and for her son Caesarion. Hearing that Octavian was on his way back to Rome, and that he considered himself Caesar's son and heir in all possible manifestations, Cleopatra undoubtedly understood that the young Caesarion, Caesar's only flesh and blood son, would be perceived as a threat by his adoptive brother. She may very well have feared for her own life as well. We don't know whether she spent her last days in Rome in hiding or what measures she took to secure her family's safety. We should not dismiss the possibility that Antony contacted Cleopatra and somehow took her under his protective wing, helping her flee safely.

As Cleopatra readied her family for flight back to Egypt, she contemplated the impact all of this profound change would have on her future ambitions. A few dagger strokes had ended her dream of ruling the world at Caesar's side, and had taken away the umbrella of security for her monarchy in Egypt. The world will never be certain what Caesar had planned for the Queen of Egypt. It may even be that for Cleopatra's career, his death was the best thing that could have happened at that time. But for now, all was uncertain and unstable, and Cleopatra knew she must go back to Egypt and take stock of the situation.

To assure herself there could be no fifth column in her midst that might be susceptible to hostile influences, she arranged to have her then fifteen-year-old husband/brother, Ptolemy XIV poisoned to death before they left Rome. Cleopatra returned to Egypt as sole and uncontested possessor of the throne, and last surviving child of Ptolemy Auletes. By the middle of April, one month after Caesar's death, Cleopatra and her son had quietly slipped out of Rome and returned home.

• Antony •

Marc Antony, the man who played the co-starring role in Cleopatra's life from the time of the great dictator's death until her own, was no Julius Caesar. The two men had in common their affairs with Cleopatra, and the rule of the Roman Empire, but in character, personality, and talent they could hardly have been more different.

Marc Antony was born in 83 B.C. a distant relative to Caesar. His family claimed to be descendant from the god Hercules. The family was not well to do, and Antony's father died when Antony was a child. The boy was raised by his mother and stepfather until the latter was ordered murdered by Cicero in 63 B.C. An unruly and rebellious teenager, Antony associated with unsavory company, and was notorious for his promiscuous, heaving drinking and free-spending habits. Tall, muscular, and handsome, Antony was a commanding physical presence. His early sexual experience included a homosexual relationship with a boy, Curio, which caused quite an upheaval in his family.

Antony may have been close to Curio more for the money than for love or sex, since Antony's debts were many and deep, and Curio had offered to pay them off!

When Antony joined the military, however, his true talents came to the fore. Quickly rising through the ranks of the cavalry, Antony proved to be a brave and gifted horseman with a flair for leadership in battle. Fighting alongside Caesar in Gaul, the older man is said to have been irritated by Antony's personality, yet impressed with his military prowess and expert command of the cavalry.

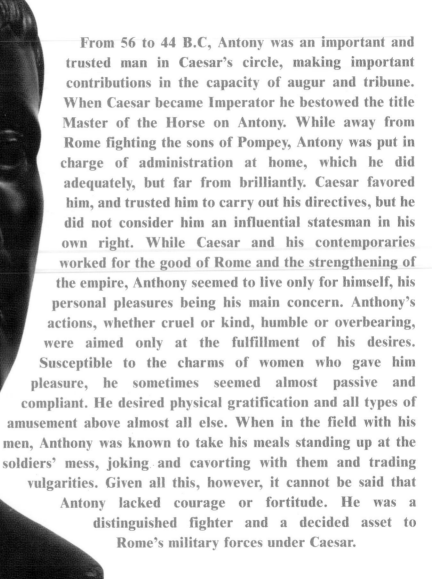

From 56 to 44 B.C, Antony was an important and trusted man in Caesar's circle, making important contributions in the capacity of augur and tribune. When Caesar became Imperator he bestowed the title Master of the Horse on Antony. While away from Rome fighting the sons of Pompey, Antony was put in charge of administration at home, which he did adequately, but far from brilliantly. Caesar favored him, and trusted him to carry out his directives, but he did not consider him an influential statesman in his own right. While Caesar and his contemporaries worked for the good of Rome and the strengthening of the empire, Anthony seemed to live only for himself, his personal pleasures being his main concern. Anthony's actions, whether cruel or kind, humble or overbearing, were aimed only at the fulfillment of his desires. Susceptible to the charms of women who gave him pleasure, he sometimes seemed almost passive and compliant. He desired physical gratification and all types of amusement above almost all else. When in the field with his men, Anthony was known to take his meals standing up at the soldiers' mess, joking and cavorting with them and trading vulgarities. Given all this, however, it cannot be said that Antony lacked courage or fortitude. He was a distinguished fighter and a decided asset to Rome's military forces under Caesar.

Rhetoric and speeches however, simply bored him. He went through the motions of attending discussions as necessary in his political position, but was never truly mentally or emotionally stimulated by the issues of the day which so preoccupied Rome. He could never have held his own with Caesar in an intellectual discourse of any kind, nor was he interested in doing so. His true loves were laughter, fun, and indulgences of all kinds.

Antony

None of this should be taken to mean however, that Anthony did not desire power! In fact, while he was not motivated by ethical and moral considerations as to what would be "good for Rome", he was most certainly interested in what was "good for Anthony" in terms of his rise up the ranks of influence. In the year 44 B.C. Caesar promoted Anthony to co-consul, making him one of the most powerful men in Rome. Previous to becoming consul, while the two worked closely together and Antony was in effect Caesar's protégé, we can't be sure if there was genuine affection between the two. Long before the actual assassination, the conspirators sounded Antony out as a possible co-conspirator; he understood their intentions, yet never bothered to warn Caesar. He must have understood all too well that Caesar's death at that particular time would put him in an advantageous position from which to launch into supreme power.

And so in the spring of 44 B.C. Cleopatra watched and listened closely for developments out of Rome. Who would be the next great leader whose affection it would be advantageous to seek? She would make no move until it was clear which of the protagonists would emerge victorious. Her rule again established in Egypt, she bided her time as the Romans struggled to reestablish the state after the death of Caesar. Through agents Cleopatra had planted in Rome, she received with great interest and excitement the reports of the struggles between Octavian and Antony.

• Antony and Cleopatra •

In the year 43 B.C. matters in Rome were finally settled to some degree when Antony and Octavian put aside their differences and formed a triumvirate with Lepidus. During this period, Cleopatra declared her son Caesarion King of Egypt and joint ruler according to the Ptolemy tradition. Rome recognized the son of Caesar as the new King, perhaps in recognition of the support of Egypt for the Triumvirate. The Republican leaders Brutus and Cassius remained the mortal enemies of all three of the Caesarian triumvirs, and battles between them were far from over. Cleopatra did not want to take sides at this point, since she feared the strength of the Republicans, and had to do some clever maneuvering in order to stay out of the struggle. When asked to send naval reinforcements to the Triumvirs, she did so, but ordered them to turn back before having to take part in battle. She had already sent four legions to the Republicans, but that had been when she was certain that Cassius about to win! When it became clear that the Triumvirs were taking the upper hand, Cleopatra chose a low profile for Egypt. The conflict raged until the great battle of Phillipi in 42 B.C. when Octavian and Antony trounced the Republicans in a decisive victory. Immediately following their defeat, Brutus and Cassius took their own lives.

After Phillipi, Lepidus faded from importance, and was given the province of Africa to govern. Antony and Octavian divided the rest of the territory under Rome between themselves. Antony took over the East, which included Egypt, and Octavian returned to Rome to administer the

Western states. Their agreement was that Antony would march his armies eastward in order to mine the wealth of the east **to replenish** now-impoverished Rome. Antony looked forward to his role, assuming that conquering the east would be no great challenge and that he would emerge the undisputed single most powerful Roman, fashioning his image after that of Caesar, and calling himself the New Dionysus.

Antony proceeded to march his legions through Greece and Asia Minor, gathering treasure on his way. His arrival in Ephesus was greeted with parades and celebration fitting the "god of joy". Those who had supported Cassius and Brutus cowered in fear, but Antony showed a great deal of humanity and pardoned almost all of the former Republicans. While in Asia Minor Antony levied heavy taxes and demanded huge sums to be paid to Rome. In a short time he became extremely unpopular and was tagged with the nickname Antony the Bloodthirsty. He lived an opulent life, thinking nothing of seizing property from the local rich and handing it over to his entourage to plunder.

Women were not scarce in Antony's company, and stories of his various mistresses reached all corners of the empire, including, of course, Egypt.

By this time it was clear to Cleopatra that Antony was the man of the hour, and she carefully planned her strategy in winning him over. By the year 41 B.C. when Antony was in Tarsus, he had already invited her several times to meet him there. Cleopatra purposefully tarried and delayed, displaying a great deal of self confidence with her "in no

Cleopatra:
...I laughed him out of patience; and that night
I laughed him into patience; and next morn,
Ere the ninth hour, I drunk him to his bed;
Then put my tires[1] and mantles on him, whilst
I wore his sword Philippan. [2]

1. headdress
2. (Antony's sword is named after Philippi, where he conquered Brutus and Cassius)

From Shakespeare: Antony and Cleopatra Act 11, scene 5

hurry" attitude. As Queen of a wealthy country and as daughter of an old ruling dynasty, Cleopatra saw herself as far more worthy of honor and respect than the many princes and leaders

of the east who had rushed to Antony's beck and call and bowed before him. She saw herself as the Egyptian people did. They worshipped her as the goddess Isis, and were in awe of their great Queen who ruled Egypt alone. She was also the mother of the only flesh and blood male child of Caesar himself. When finally she did agree to a meeting, it would be on her own terms, and it would be characteristically creative, daring, and decisive.

Cleopatra was well aware that Antony intended to continue to march his armies to the East, with Egypt his eventual destination. She knew too, that her country could do little to resist him. Her throne was in a very precarious position. If Antony decided to take over Egypt for Rome he would certainly be able to do so.

So the Queen studied her options, learned as much as she could about the propensities and habits of this Roman leader, and quietly planned her next maneuvers. A great deal of Cleopatra's genius was in her impeccable sense of timing. She knew that, as it had been with Caesar, the first meeting with Antony would make or break her chances with the man. When at last she felt she'd put Antony off long enough, she set out on her bold journey to meet him.

Cleopatra readied a large fleet of ships filled with expensive gifts, and set said for Tarsus. As she traversed the Mediterranean she and her servants prepared a barge for the grand surprise she would present to Antony upon arrival. They equipped the barge with splendid purple sails and its oars were gilded with silver. When they neared Tarsus, Cleopatra arranged herself on a gorgeous golden recliner, surrounded with boys like cupids fanning her. Great quantities of incense were burned upon the barge, sending seductive scent wafting onto the shores. Cleopatra arranged herself in the pose of Aphrodite, and lay beneath a golden canopy. Musicians played lutes and string instruments as the oarsmen gently rowed the barge toward the shore.

A brilliant plan! Cleopatra presented herself as goddess meeting god! Aphrodite arriving to meet Dionysus! After all, Cleopatra must surely have known about Antony's own arrival in Ephesus, and by arriving thus as a goddess she put herself on equal footing with the leader.

Crowds gathered on the banks as word of mouth flew through the marketplace announcing a strange and beautiful sight on the water. The silvery oars shimmered as the barge approached, revealing the sight of

Enobarbus:
… Cleopatra, catching but the least noise of this, dies[1] instantly; I have seen her die twenty times upon far poorer moment.[2] I do think there is mettle[3] in death, which commits some loving act upon her, she hath such celerity in dying.

Antony:
She is cunning past man's thought.

Enobarbus:
Alack, sir, no; her passions are made of nothing but the finest part of pure love. We cannot call her winds and waters sighs and tears; they are greater storms and tempests than almanacs can report. This cannot be cunning in her; if it be, she makes a show'r of rain as well as Jove.

1. (throughout his speech Enobarbus puns on a second meaning of die, "to experience sexual orgasm")
2. cause
3. strength

From Shakespeare: Antony and Cleopatra Act 1, scene 2

the Queen reclining comfortably and regally. Antony, however, did not at first see this spectacle. He heard the rumors, and knew what was taking place, but remained in the marketplace where he was holding judicial meetings. He sent a messenger to the Queen asking her to meet him later to dine. Cleopatra cleverly kept the advantage on her side by countering with an invitation to Antony to dine with her on her barge. Since by now it was clear to Antony that the Queen would not be coming to the marketplace to boy at his feet, he agreed. When Antony did arrive, the reception Cleopatra offered was lavish and impressive, sparing nothing.

There can be no doubt that Cleopatra accomplished a brilliant coup with her first meeting with Antony. We don't know whether they became lovers immediately as was the case with Caesar, and perhaps since Cleopatra was now a bit older and wiser she held back strategically. Antony entertained the Queen the following night with a banquet of his own, which rivaled hers in sumptuous extravagance, although his artfulness as gracious host left much to be desired. Cleopatra had plenty of opportunity over the first two days in Tarsus to demonstrate to Antony her womanly appeal as well as her wit and intelligence. Antony must have known he was in the presence of one who excelled in both areas, while his own tastes were perhaps more primitive, and his intellect and will no match for hers. Realizing her superiority in both mind and character, he fell in love with, and very much under the influence of Cleopatra. Antony was then 42 years old, and Cleopatra was 27.

The relationship between Cleopatra and Antony was quite different

than that between the Queen and the deceased imperator. Cleopatra was adept at conforming her demeanor to the person with whom she dealt. With Caesar, himself a man of culture and great intellect, Cleopatra spoke demurely and behaved in a refined manner. With Antony however, she soon adapted her own mannerisms to his, and influenced him perhaps to the point of exploitation, by using his weaknesses and inferior mind to hers to control him.

By all accounts, however, Antony was deeply in love with Cleopatra, whereas Caesar's affections probably did not reach that level of commitment.

One of the first demonstrations of Cleopatra's over Antony was the execution of Arsinoe, Cleopatra's hated sister. Caesar had not agreed to do away with her, and the two women were now the only survivors of the children of Ptolemy XIII. Antony readily agreed to have Arsinoe killed, to the great satisfaction of his mistress. Antony went even further, and gifted the Queen with the island of Cyprus. He also ordered killed a would-be king who claimed to be the drowned King Ptolemy XIII. This left Cleopatra and her son, as the only surviving offspring of the Ptolemy line, securely on the throne of Egypt.

Over the course of her visit in Tarsus, Cleopatra accomplished what she had set out to do, and much more. She seems to have had no trouble convincing Antony of her innocence regarding her lack of support for the Triumvirs, claiming weather conditions as the reason her navy had turned back. More importantly, perhaps, she succeeded in winning Antony over to the idea that without Egypt's strength and wealth, and more particularly, without her as sovereign Queen of Egypt, he would be in a weakened position against Octavian. As demonstration of Egypt's great wealth, Cleopatra is said to have wagered with Antony that she would be willing to spend a huge sum on one meal. Antony being a gambling man (as Cleopatra had no doubt already known), he took the bet and the Queen provided an inarguably extravagant and luxurious spread. However, when doubt was expressed as to the actual sum she had spent on the meal, Cleopatra removed her pearl earring, had it assessed by Antony's experts who declared it worth more than the sum in question. This pearl she put into a cup of water, and consumed. No more graphic demonstration could have been

planned to convince the Roman of the vast wealth of her country and of her willingness to put it as his disposal (if her own demands were met as well, of course.)

By the time the Queen left Tarsus Antony was smitten with her as a woman, and tied to her in political alliance as well. Cleopatra returned to Alexandria satisfied and gratified that her plan had more than succeeded. Her throne was secure and she was again mistress to the most powerful man in Rome.

• Antony in Alexandria •

A year of separation followed the first meeting of Antony and Cleopatra. Antony spent the time tending to matters in Palestine and Syria where Rome's holdings were reorganized and secured. Cleopatra quietly minded affairs in Egypt, while waiting for the Roman to make his appearance. In late autumn of the year 41 B.C. Antony finally did arrive in Alexandria.

By all accounts, Antony surrendered himself to a sort of extended vacation while in Egypt. Antony's conquests of the East had been achieved without serious conflict, and he apparently thought he could now rest on his laurels, taking the winter of 41-40 B.C. as a respite from duties of any kind.

Letting all matters of state slide, he indulged in a life of pleasure with his mistress, enjoying banquets, gambling, drinking, and all manner of entertainment.

While his seeming indifference to politics during this period may well have distressed Cleopatra, she was Antony's willing partner in feasting, hunting and fishing, as well as his ever delightful sexual partner, and never lost sight of the need to strengthen her hold on the Roman. The Queen indulged in pastimes otherwise not to her own tastes and liking, in order to spend more time with Antony and bind him closer to him. While we can never be sure of her true feelings toward Antony, there is no question that she contrived to keep him under her influence, using whatever means she deemed necessary, and that she read his needs and desires, using them masterfully for her purposes. By keeping his desire for her fresh and by seeing to it that his every desire was taken care of, the Queen kept Antony firmly in her web. Whether she kept the love fires burning solely for her own political purposes or whether she was stirred by some affection for the man, we shall never be certain.

Cleopatra was seen playing dice and other gambling games, drinking more than was her habit, and accompanying him when he exercised. Together the two would even play practical jokes on the citizenry, disguised as slaves at night, which Antony found amusing. Once, having seen Antony order servants to affix large fish to his line during an unsuccessful fishing trip, Cleopatra played a prank on Antony whereby she had small herring which was not native to the lake they fished put on his line. Antony laughed, knowing how to take a joke as well as to make them.

All that winter the pair cavorted in Cleopatra's magnificent court in Alexandria. Her palaces were grand and luxurious, and life in the city was peaceful and charming. The pull of this voluptuous lifestyle on Antony was palpable, and suited his tastes to perfection. He even dressed in Greek attire; something the Romans looked down upon as an embarrassment. Antony was not base or corrupt, and his behavior was rarely cruel. His childish exuberance for life and his insatiable appetite for pleasure were what motivated him. Against the most pleasing lifestyle he'd attained in Egypt with Cleopatra, the pleas of Rome that for the triumvir's return had no chance of being heard. Indeed, the numerous messages received by Antony in Alexandria begging him to come back were returned unanswered. Antony adopted Alexandria as a sort of second home, living there as a distinguished guest, rather than as a ruling general, as had Caesar. Although Roman legions were in Egypt with Antony, and Caesarion was co-ruler in name, Cleopatra was clearly in charge.

While Cleopatra and Antony enjoyed their winter of peace and decadence, Rome underwent another period of upheaval. Fulvia, Antony's legal wife, who had remained in Rome while her husband marched to the east and then sojourned with his mistress, had been stirring up trouble against Octavian. There had been until then an uneasy alliance between Antony and Octavian, and Fulvia, along with Antony's brother Lucius, raised tensions into a campaign against the younger Triumvir. Fulvia's was motivated by a desire to force her husband back home, and away from her hated rival, Cleopatra, as much as by desire to overthrow Octavian. Although Octavian was quickly gaining the upper hand against his wife and brother, still Antony did not move from his comfortable lair in Alexandria.

Caesar and Pompey "knew" Cleopatra when she was very young and she did not yet understand the ways of the world. When she went to Antonius, her beauty, as well as her judgment, were at their prime. Therefore, she equipped herself with lots of gold and silver, riches and ornaments that were suitable from such a wealthy realm as Egypt was. However, what she trusted in most, was not any of these riches, but in herself, and in the charms of her beauty and grace. Therefore, when she received letters from Antonius himself and his friends, she mocked him so much that she would only see him in her finest pomp and glory. She went down the river on her barge whose poop was of gold, the sails purple, and the oars were of silver. The oars kept time to the music that was played on the barge by many instruments. She herself was laid under a tent made of gold cloth, dressed like the goddess Venus (as commonly depicted in the painting), and attended by pretty boys dressed as painters depict Cupid – with little fans with which they fanned her. She was also attended by ladies (some dressed

• Antony leaves Egypt •

Something did soon rouse Antony to action, finally. The Parthians had meanwhile been raiding Syria and Asia Minor and having little difficulty overcoming those territories, where Antony had left a weak system in place.

In Judea, the Parthians captured Jerusalem and forced Herod to take refuge on Mount Massada. These provinces were falling one by one due to Antony's neglect. Antony, realizing he must set out to right matters, finally left his mistress and adopted land in the spring of 40 B.C. He traveled to Tyre, one of the only cities to resist the Parthian onslaught, and from there he journeyed to Greece.

Meanwhile, Lucius lost to Octavian in Perusia, and his armies were massacred. Fulvia then fled to Athens to meet her husband. Their reunion could not have been a very happy one, since Fulvia was full of bitterness and anger over Antony's relationship with the Cleopatra, and Antony was angry at his wife's instigation of civil war against

like the nymphs Nereides – mermaids of the water) who steered the helm and tended the tackle and ropes of the barge. From the barge, wafted the sweet fragrances of perfumes which even reached the banks. The multitudes of people on the banks either ran along with the barge, or ran to the city to see her coming in. Antonius was left alone on his imperial seat in the marketplace to give audience. When Cleopatra landed, Antonius invited her for supper, but she invited him to her for supper instead. Antonius was happy to be courteous and accepted her invitation to supper – where he found such delicious food that it can't be described. However, he was most impressed by the infinite number of lights and devices that gave light everywhere. The next night, Antonius tried to surpass her in magnificence and finery, but she overcame him in both.

From Plutarch
"Life of Marcus Antonius" in The Lives of the Noble Grecians and Romans

Octavian. During their short time together Fulvia fell seriously ill, but Antony left her and moved on towards Rome. He had raised a considerable army in the meantime, and they laid siege to Brundisium and made ready to battle Octavian's forces. Before a fresh outbreak of hostilities could begin, however, word arrived that Fulvia had passed away.

Antony, on hearing this news, bent in grief, and was overcome with remorse that in his anger, he had neglected even to bid her good-bye. He lost his will to fight, and Octavian too, was willing to lay down his arms since Fulvia, the instigator of the war, was gone. The two reconciled again, reinstating the Triumvirate. Lepidus retained control of Africa, and Octavian and Antony divided the eastern and western holdings between them in more exact detail previously. Antony was given the entire East, including Greece, Macedonia, Asia, and Syria. Octavian controlled the European provinces. Egypt was still considered an independent kingdom, and

Italy was a neutral homeland where the generals could train forces for campaigns in all sectors. In actuality, however, Octavian retained control at home.

Since Antony now was legally a widower, he was open to a political marriage, and was soon pressed to wed Octavia, the younger sister of Octavian. This marriage symbolized a coming together of the two sides, and held out the hope of a lasting peace. It was hoped in Rome, that by marrying the Triumvir to an attractive Roman woman he would forget his luxurious life in Alexandria, and remain closer to home, taking up his political duties in a responsible matter. Though the marriage was not his initiative, by all accounts Antony put up very little resistance to the idea, and his feeble objections concerning Cleopatra held little sway. Octavian held military superiority at the time despite his stated desire to put aside hostilities, so Antony had little choice but to bow to Octavian's wish that the marriage take place. The marriage cemented the written agreement between the Triumvirs.

Octavia was a beautiful woman, probably far more so than Cleopatra, and also a bit younger. She was far from as forceful a personality however, and certainly did not possess the wiles and manipulative mind of her husband's mistress. She was of noble character, and steadfastly endured at her husband's side, even when that meant humiliation and pain. Octavia had been married previously, and was herself a fresh widow. She was pregnant with her former husband's child at the time of her wedding to Antony.

• Cleopatra waits •

Cleopatra too, was with child, and in fact gave birth to Antony's offspring – twins – only a few weeks before the wedding of Octavia and Antony. The twins, a boy and a girl, were named Alexander Helios and Cleopatra Selene. As jubilant as the Romans were about Antony's new marriage, Cleopatra was surely as despondent. The fact that she had born Antony two children was overshadowed by his marriage of political convenience to a seemingly able foe. Cleopatra feared for that all of her efforts of the previous winter had after all been for naught. Would she still have the protection and support of Rome now that Antony was married to the sister of his rival triumvir? Would Egypt now be vulnerable to takeover as a Roman province?

Cleopatra knew of Octavia, her beauty and grace, and her position in society in Rome. She knew that Octavia would fight to preserve her marriage, if not only out of love of Antony, then for love of her brother, and her desire to see peace in Rome and in her family. Cleopatra resolved not to allow this worthy rival to usurp her own powerful position as woman of Antony's heart. She would use her considerable determination, will, and energy to ensure her return to the role of woman behind the man. Cleopatra would not long agree to be preempted by the likes of a Roman wife. Antony was still her only hope for power and glory, and she would not easily give up her dream.

Did Antony miss Cleopatra? Did he think of her at all? There is no evidence that he contacted her at all during his absence, so we have no way of knowing for sure. We can only guess whether at that point Cleopatra remained in his mind a forgettable interlude or whether he had plans or hopes ever to renew their liaison. We do not even know how Antony felt about his twin children born in Egypt, one being a male child, when Octavia produced only daughters.

The lovers were to be separated for a total of almost four years. During that time, Cleopatra did not sit idle and give up her influence on the man who was her hope for might and glory. She kept close watch on Antony by way of a web of undercover agents she had placed in Rome, and later in Greece. Antony's every move was reported to the Queen, who not only planted those who would provide information, but also those who could act, surreptitiously, on her behalf. The most oft-reported example of this is the incident of the soothsayer whom Cleopatra apparently commissioned to tell Antony that the stars were warning him to stay far away from Octavian.

During the first year following Antony's marriage to Octavia, he stayed at home in Rome. The relationship Antony shared with his brother-in-law was fraught with jealousies and petty rivalries. Though this period was for the most part peaceful, the differences in character and style between the two were too striking to allow a true friendship to deepen, and they never truly go along. When Antony lost, as he often did, in dice or other games, he would become annoyed and angry, and resentment built which each incident.

Octavia

Yet it was Antony who had the affections of the people of Rome. Though a generation older than Octavian, Antony's boyish energy and exuberance, along with his physical strength and prowess were much admired. The pale and serious Octavian was no match for Antony's charms. But while he may not have captured the people's affection, Octavian was far from the weaker of the two, for his mind was as sharp and effective as his body was feeble. Time would show how this would stand Octavian in good stead, while Antony wasted his gifts on excess and indulgence.

Octavian

In 39 B.C. Antony traveled to Greece and took up residence in Athens along with his wife. His lifestyle in Athens was similar to the one he'd had in Alexandria two years earlier. Concerned chiefly with the luxuries and sensual pleasures of life, he again neglected the administrative duties and work connected with the ruling of an empire. It cannot be charged then, that Cleopatra was the influence which dictated his priorities in Egypt. The fact that he carried on in similar manner while married to

Octavia points to his own character and tastes being responsible for such behavior. To underwrite his escapades Antony oppressed the Greeks financially, taxing them exorbitantly, and extorting large sums of money from them at every turn.

While Antony feasted in Greece, he sent his armies to Asia Minor and Syria to oust the Parthians, and these campaigns were successfully carried out. Antony celebrated the victories in grand style, but as usual he then neglected to invest any thought and effort into the administration and security of those areas of his empire. When his general, Ventidius, who had succeeded in a great conquest over the Parthians, was the hero of the day in Rome, Antony was overcome by jealousy, and ordered Ventidius home in order to assure he'd have no more military successes! Antony himself then took his place as commander of the Roman armies in Syria. When Antony took over he undid some of Ventidius' gains when he was forced to make peace with the besieged king in Samasota for far less a sum than had already been offered to his general! After this humiliation, to which Antony paid scant attention, he returned to Athens to take up his former lifestyle there.

The next year was the last of the present Triumvirate agreement, and as the expiration drew near, tensions increased between Antony and Octavian. More than once, civil war seemed inevitable, and then was brought back from the brink. In the spring of 37 B.C. Antony was in Rome, negotiating the third Triumvirate. The mediating efforts of Octavia played a major role in the outcome of the negotiations and final signing of the agreement. Octavia's personal stake was great, since she stood to lose the affections of either her brother or her husband by taking sides in their conflict. She argued to Octavian that should he not ally with her husband he would be causing great grief to her and her children, since Antony would surely then turn against her and return to his former lover in Egypt. Perhaps she feared that Antony was tiring of a wife who disapproved of his drinking and other irksome habits and pined for his mistress who never rebuked him, but joined merrily with him with no encouragement needed. In the end the agreement was forged, and the Triumvirate set for another five year period.

● Antony and Cleopatra Again ●

Octavian turned his attention to his enemies in the west, and along with his faithful general Agrippa, prepared his armies confront Sextus Pompey. Antony again set his sails for Greece, taking his wife, Octavia with him only as far as Corfu, where he sent her back to Rome with the explanation that in her pregnant condition (she was expecting her third child with Anthony, the first two being girls) she should not be traveling, and that he would be preparing for further war against the Parthians, which would be dangerous for her. Antony seemed already to have decided to ally himself again with the Egyptian Queen during his eastern adventures, and dispatched Octavia back to Rome in order to get her out of the way.

As he journeyed toward Syria, Antony sent word to Cleopatra to meet him there with their two children who were now nearly four years old.

Why did Antony "suddenly" decide to defect from his marriage and Rome and turn again toward the Egypt and Cleopatra? Was it only that Octavia had become a tiresome companion and his heart again yearned for the passion and laughter he'd enjoyed in Alexandria? We should not readily assume that Antony had pined for his former mistress and finally could no longer stand being separated from her. Some accounts do declare that Antony harbored a secret passion for Cleopatra during their separation which burned ever stronger as he traveled east. However, Antony never lacked for female company outside his marriage to Octavia and had few qualms about marrying her just after Cleopatra had birthed him two children. It is more likely that "out of sight, out of mind" applied to his feelings for Cleopatra at that point. Neither should we assume that his marriage to Octavia was full of love or affection. However, if at one time it had behooved him politically to marry Octavia, then now the Egyptian Queen could be just as satisfactory a match for similar reasons. Perhaps he realized that he was in great need of the riches of Egypt, as well as the astute mind and counsel of his former lover? Egypt would make a fine backup for his campaign against the Parthians, and Alexandria would be capital of the entire East. As supreme ruler in the area he may have felt the weight of his responsibilities and longed for a woman who could function as political partner as well as bed-partner. The possibility remains of course, that in addition to these concerns, indeed Antony did miss Cleopatra, and that finally an opportune moment to reunite with her had presented itself, which he would not squander.

Cleopatra made her way to Syria with a glad and optimistic heart. Antony was now even more powerful and in control of more of the Roman Empire than ever before. He was in a position to make Cleopatra an extremely powerful woman and to see that her son by Caesar, and his own two

children were set up to inherit large portions of the empire and perhaps kingdoms of their own. She surely realized that with Antony she had far more chance than she'd ever had with Caesar to realize her dreams of being Empress of Rome and ruling side by side with the most powerful man in the world. Caesar likely never envisioned her, and did not need her, as a full partner in that sense, while Antony was far more pliable and would be more easily persuaded to advance Cleopatra's goals as his own.

Indeed, soon after Cleopatra's arrival in Antioch, Antony announced the presentation of large territorial gifts to her and the children. She received almost the entire Mediterranean coastal area, Cyprus, and Crete. Caesarion was recognized by Antony as heir to the Empire! This made Cleopatra sovereign over far vaster holdings than any Ptolemy Pharaoh had ruled before her. She was well on her way to realizing her ambition that Egypt would become a major power.

Rome boiled with anger! That an Egyptian woman had duped them out of so much of the Empire was unthinkable. Cleopatra was seen in Rome as an evil sorceress, rather than as a brave and remarkable leader who had maintained and expanded her position against terrible odds. Rome was incensed as well that Antony's legitimate children by Octavia had been ignored, while Cleopatra's children had received such generous dispensation. Antony himself, however, saw nothing shameful in having children with his mistress, and clearly claimed paternity of the twins. In fact, in his mind they constituted more evidence likening him to his proclaimed ancestor Hercules, who had fathered numerous children with several women. To Antony, this pointed to his outstanding vitality and virility, not to immorality. Like Hercules, Antony saw himself as being governed not by the laws of men, but by a supernatural law where anything was allowed.

Octavian, in particular, was not pleased by the news that his partner Triumvir had parted so recklessly with strategic parts of the empire. Their already precarious relationship was further strained by this news. Antony, as was his wont, was complacent in the face of all this disapproval and failed to take it seriously. Antony's indifference to Rome's reaction only served to further incense Octavian who deeply resented this public humiliation of his sister.

At some point during their sojourn in Syria, there took place, by many accounts, a marriage of the Triumvir to the Queen, although exact details of this event have not come down through history. If they did have an actual formal wedding, this would have been perfectly legal in Egyptian terms, and as far as the East was concerned, Cleopatra was then legally wedded to Antony. In Rome, of course, Antony's marriage to Octavia was still legally binding. There could have been no logical reason for Antony to desire an actual marriage to Cleopatra, so if a wedding did actually take place it is evidence that Cleopatra was able to wield power and influence over the man and to persuade him to do her bidding. No official announcement of Antony's marriage to Cleopatra was recorded in Rome. And Egypt never proclaimed Antony King.

Octavia

Antony, Cleopatra and the children spent the winter of 37 – 36 B.C. in Antioch, the third largest Mediterranean city at that time. Antony was occupied largely with preparations for his upcoming military campaign against the Parthians. He raised a huge and impressive army of over one hundred thousand men, the largest army ever to fight in the East for Rome. The entire world was poised in suspense as it awaited a battle which could change the face of Asia.

When Antony began to march his armies toward Parthia in March, 36 B.C, Cleopatra was at his side. The world watched with great anticipation as Antony advanced, the fact that Cleopatra supported him and approved of his campaign was plain for all to see. By association with the mightiest of men, she herself was able to wield power of her own. During the first part of the march, Cleopatra discovered that she was again pregnant with a child by Antony. When Antony's armies reached the Euphrates, Cleopatra parted company with him, whether at Antony's insistence or her own initiative.

Antony (to Cleopatra):
Fie, wrangling queen!
Whom everything becomes – to
   chide, to laugh,
To weep: whose every passion fully[1]
   strives
To make itself, in thee, fair and
   admired….

1. absolutely and successfully

**From Shakespeare: Antony and Cleopatra
Act 1, scene 1**

On her way back to Alexandria, the Queen traveled from Damascus to the Sea of Galilee, and then south to Jericho, to view some coveted Judean land which Antony had recently bestowed upon her. Both the gift of land and Cleopatra's visit caused much consternation to King Herod of Judea. Herod hated and mistrusted the Queen and resented her having been gifted with such a rich area of his kingdom. By some accounts Cleopatra endeavored to seduce Herod. If this was true, we can deduce that her supposed ardor for the King was an act, aimed at getting her something she desired. It hardly seems likely that she would betray Antony, whose child she was presently carrying, and who was the most important man in the world, in order to carry on with Herod, whom up until that time she had despised and tried to convince Antony to drive from his throne! Herod, in fact seemed to have seen through her cunning act, and he rejected her advances. He even seriously considered doing away with her, believing he would be doing the world a favor by putting to death a dangerous and cunning woman who wielded too much power. In the end he decided against that plan, when his advisors convinced him that Antony would certainly avenge the Queen's murder, even if he believed she had been trying to betray him. Thus both Herod and Cleopatra played at hiding their hatred for one another – she by pretending passion, and he with politeness and flattery.

By the time Cleopatra departed Judea, a deal had been struck whereby Herod would lease back the fertile groves near Jericho which were now under her possession. At the conclusion of their business, Herod accompanied Cleopatra to Pelusium, at the border of Egypt, and they continued their friendly charade as he offered her splendid gifts and bade her have a safe journey home. Cleopatra and her company then continued the journey toward Alexandria. Once back at the royal palace, the queen resumed her sovereign duties and awaited her confinement, which took place some months later. She bore a son, her fourth child, and her third by Antony, whom she called Ptolemy Philadelphus. Thus settled into domestic bliss, Cleopatra awaited news, which she was sure would soon arrive, of Antony's great victories against the Parthians.

Antony:
…I must from this enchanting[1] queen break off…

1. spellbinding

From Shakespeare: Antony and Cleopatra Act 1, scene 2

• Antony Disappoints •

Alas, the news which did arrive was quite different from what had been expected. A year passed during which Antony experienced failure after failure. He marched his troops for five months in hard conditions, dragging gigantic equipment including a huge battering ram, which in the end he was forced to abandon before having opportunity to put it to use. The Parthian campaign ended in complete disaster and defeat. Besieged not only by the Parthians but also by famine and lack of morale, the greatest army Rome had ever raised was in shambles, having lost thousands upon thousands of men, and was in retreat.

In the winter of 36 B.C. Antony sent up a desperate call from Syria for Cleopatra save him from his predicament. He sent plea after impassioned plea for his mistress to shore him up with troops and provisions. While waiting for her response the Triumvir resorted to old habits of drink and moody despondency. Day after day he gazed out to sea, hoping to see the Egyptian fleet nearing the shores of Phoenicia where he impatiently and drunkenly bided his time.

Due to events she could not have envisioned, and certainly did not desire, Cleopatra was now actually in a more powerful position than her lover, as Antony was dependent upon her as never before. When at last Cleopatra sent a fleet to reinforce the failed Roman army, it was several months after the first requests had reached her. She accompanied her army in order to be with Antony and take stock of the situation herself. When she finally came ashore to greet Antony she was undoubtedly quite shocked at what she found. Antony was a tired and broken man, surrounded

by hungry and depleted armies. He gratefully distributed the food and supplies she had brought for the troops, and did not deride her for bringing very little money. For money he resorted to extortion of funds from the kings and princes still under his control. With this he paid his soldiers, telling them that the money was a gift from Cleopatra. With this declaration he hoped to present her in a positive light and increase her prestige in Rome. The queen herself, no doubt bitterly disappointed in the way things had turned out, could hardly have helped comparing the defeated Antony with Caesar, knowing that in the same circumstances Caesar would have trounced the Parthians and history would have played out quite differently.

She was always finding new delights for Antonius, never leaving his side night or day. She would play dice with him, drink with him, hunt with him, and be with him when he exercised.

From Plutarch
"Life of Marcus Antonius" in The Lives of the Noble Grecians and Romans

• Octavian Rising •

At the same time that Antony's military adventures were winding down in disgrace, Octavian was experiencing brilliant victories elsewhere in the West. In addition to driving Sextus Pompey from Sicily, he had taken over control of the African provinces which had previously been assigned to Lepidus, the third Triumvir, thus canceling his influence, and for all intents leaving only Antony and himself administering the Roman Empire. Octavian was hailed in Roman senate for his amazing feats of strategy, having overturned his previous reputation for being somewhat of a weakling! Octavian's position in Rome brought about a new feeling of stability, the feeling among the senators and the nobility was that perhaps Octavian would be able to improve social conditions and they looked to him to reorganize matters at home.

Although officially Antony and Octavian were still partners and co-rulers of the empire, the latter was starting to plot the final confrontation. In fact, Octavian probably never ceased to regard Antony as his enemy and had strategically waited for the right time to come for him to make his move against him.

While Rome celebrated Octavian's conquests, Antony had to be content with the fact that he still did control the eastern provinces, his failure against the Parthians notwithstanding. He no doubt consoled himself with the fact of his alliance with Egypt, an extremely wealthy country, whose armies were now at his disposal. Meanwhile, the Roman army in Syria licked its wounds and shored itself up with the help of the Egyptian reinforcements Cleopatra had brought. Of course, Antony did not report his adventures to Rome as failure – quite the contrary. In his reports to the Senate he managed to turn defeat into victory and retreat into triumph! Octavian officially celebrated Antony's activities, while secretly harboring resentment and fury toward him. Reports of what had really happened had reached Rome by other avenues, but festivals and triumphal celebrations were nevertheless held in Antony's honor! Clearly, however, the two had ceased to be partners in any sense, and the world was divided between the two, their destinies and ambitions tied up in their respective sides of the empire. Antony planned to reengage the Parthians in an effort to erase his previous disgrace, while Octavian plotted the eventual total overthrow of his brother-in-law and conquering of the east for himself.

• A Woman Scorned •

Antony and Cleopatra had repaired to Alexandria in the spring of 35 B.C., where they again established a common home. It had been two years since Antony had sent his wife back to Rome, but Octavia had far from forgotten that she was the legal mate of the Triumvir, and mother to his legitimate children. Uncharacteristically, Octavia was now ready to take bold action in an effort to bring her husband back to her, and back to Rome. We cannot be sure whether Octavia was motivated more by affection and longing for Antony or by her brother, Octavian's ambitions. Octavian desired to reel Antony in from the East and reclaim him and all that was his for Rome. He probably wished to make one last try at using the leverage of his sister's marriage to his rival to get Antony to tow the line. Octavia was extremely displeased with the reality that her husband was ensconced once again in Egypt with his former lover, whom she despised, and was happy to go along with her brother's plans.

Octavian outfitted a convoy of ships with a well-equipped bodyguard of two thousand men, along with ample money and gifts – all meant for Antony. Octavia sailed off to Greece hoping to present her husband with this bounty.

Everything was planned to flatter Antony and to lure him back to the arms of his wife and the bosom of Rome.

appointed an unrenowned man to the job. He had no wish to install Alexandra's son to an office in such proximity to his own, thereby giving the family a foothold from which to act against him. Alexandra was furious. The post of High Priest had for generations been held by members of her family, and she was determined to put matters right. Assuming that she would find a kindred spirit in Cleopatra, Alexandra sent urgent entreaties to the Egyptian Queen asking for her help. She counted on Cleopatra's hatred of Herod, and her influence over the Triumvir to overturn the previous appointment and instate her son. The entire scenario was appealing to Cleopatra on many levels. She did indeed have much in common with the aims of Alexandra. The story had elements of intrigue, which she enjoyed, and she saw a chance to support an effort to topple Herod and reinstate the Maccabees to power in Judea. She brought the issue to Antony's attention and requested his intervention to advance Alexandra's request.

Antony, in a rare show of independent thought, resisted Cleopatra and acted according to his own feelings on the matter. He either feared or respected Herod, or both, and saw no reason to force a confrontation with him at this time over his choice of High Priest. He denied Cleopatra's request to intervene directly, but as a sort of concession, agreed to meet with Aristobulus, who was a teenager, if he could be brought to Egypt to state his case directly. Herod balked at this invitation, fearing that by allowing Aristobulus to travel to Alexandria he would be exposing him to Cleopatra and the two would team up against him. Together, he reasoned, they could surely influence Antony to support the Maccabees after all. Refusing to send Aristobulus, he placed him under house arrest in his palace along with his mother. He now considered the two his direst enemies.

Looks Aren't Everything

What did Cleopatra look like, anyway? Well, that's hard to say. Twentieth century plays and movies have cast the most beautiful leading ladies of the times in the role of the great Queen. This certainly lends strength to the popular legend that Cleopatra was a striking beauty capable of bringing the most powerful men to their knees by simply being in their presence. But was it really Cleopatra's physical beauty that gave her power?

When Octavian took over Egypt he ordered all likenesses of the former Queen destroyed, and for all intents and purposes this dictate was carried out. Fortunately however, one wealthy Alexandrian citizen managed to bribe officials and kept a portion of his Cleopatra collection. Thus we have two statues (on display in a California Museum), some coins found later on, and an engraving on the wall of the Temple of Dendahra in Qena from which to approximate an image of the woman. The engraved picture shows Cleopatra nursing the baby

Alexandra would not stay quiet for long, and soon tried to execute a plot so reminiscent of Cleopatra's first meeting with Caesar that it practically announces itself as the fruit of the Egyptian Queen's fertile mind. Aristobulus and his mother were smuggled out of the palace in coffins, and were to sail to Alexandria aboard a merchant vessel! Herod's spies informed him of the plot in time, and he caught the two before they were put aboard ship. Out of fear of retribution from Cleopatra perhaps, or out of a wish to end the entire episode, Herod relented and not only did not turn Alexandra and her son into authentic corpses, but agreed to appoint Prince Aristobulus to High Priest, as they wished.

As was customary, a feast day was held to confirm Aristobulus' appointment. The day's entertainment included games of all sorts and the seventeen year old Aristobulus took part in the acrobatics shows. When the young prince, overheated from his acrobatic efforts, decided to go for a swim with a group of others his age, some of the boys played at dunking one another under the water, and when the prince was pushed under he never came up alive.

Though Herod acted devastated by the young man's death, his mother-in-law was certain that her son had fallen victim of a vicious meticulously planned murder orchestrated by Herod himself. Alexandra immediately appealed again to Cleopatra, this time begging her for help in bringing Herod to trial for the killing of Aristobulus. Antony did agree to summon Herod to meet him, but rather than in Egypt, the meeting took place in Syria where Antony was supposedly preparing his troops for another push against the Parthians. Cleopatra had remained behind in Alexandria and was not able to influence Antony's reaction to Herod's explanations of the events. The two men met as friends; Herod was quickly acquitted by the Triumvir, and no trial was held.

Antony was in dire need of some military or diplomatic success to shore up his flagging reputation in Rome. He announced his intention to

Caesarion, and she is a depicted as a lovely figure indeed. The coins and statues, however show a plump woman, with a severe face, bad teeth, and large, rounded features. These images have caused many historians to claim that the legend of Cleoaptra's "beauty" is completely unsubstantiated, and that actually she was a plain woman, perhaps even quite plump and probably no more than five feet tall. British researchers have even gone so far as to call Cleopatra "ugly"!

What supposedly drove the great leaders mad with desire, then, if not Cleopatra's repudiated ravishing appearance? Well, for one thing, beauty is a subjective quality which changes with the ages. It is well documented that in Cleopatra's time, women with rounded figures were considered ideal, and that a beautiful face was one with clear skin and bright eyes. So perhaps then, she was truly beautiful. More likely, however, and more encouraging for women everywhere and feminists especially, Cleopatra's story seems to

pit his armies against the Parthians once more, but in a surprise move, he instead invaded Armenia, a fairly defenseless state which he knew he could overrun easily. While the Armenian King had previously suspected that he was the object of Antony's next campaign, he was defenseless to stop the onslaught. Antony lured the King to his camp under pretense of negotiations, and had him chained. The Romans proceeded to plunder the King's land, destroying anything in their path which might contain gold they could extract, including statues of gods, ancient temples and artifacts. In little time, the rag-tag Armenian army was beaten into submission, and all of the Armenian treasure was in Roman hands. Armenia was thus annexed to the Roman Empire as a province.

Antony then turned to diplomatic means to annex another area. The betrothal of the daughter of the King of Media to Antony and Cleopatra's son Alexander Helios was peacefully arranged. The boy was to become the King of Media, since the present King had no sons. Antony boasted of this important alliance to Rome, along with his Armenian conquest, and expected accolades, which indeed, had he returned to Rome to celebrate his victories, he may have received. Instead, however, Antony and his armies repaired to Egypt, where an event was held that caused the world to catch its breath in surprise.

substantiate the belief that "beauty is only skin deep"! While her looks were rarely touted in the historical literature, there can be no doubt whatsoever that she possessed great charm, wit and intelligence! It was these attributes, and a knowledge of seductive strategy, perhaps, that she used to control and manipulate powerful male leaders. Cleopatra was knowledgable in military and political matters and made herself an indespensible advisor to both Caesar and Antony. In addition, she made sure in both cases that the man's first impression would be dramatic, and she seduced each one with theatrical flourish after careful planning and forethought. These were not chance meetings where the man was swept off his feet, but maticulously planned, goal oriented encounters. The Queen knew exactly what she wanted and how to go about getting it. While physical beauty couldn't have hurt, for Cleopatra, it was simply not necessary.

● Triumph on Foreign Soil ●

When he returned from battle, Antony staged a celebration, held in Alexandria, which resembled in almost all respects a Roman triumph! With this act he broke with a long and revered Roman tradition, and struck a blow at Rome's dignity and honor. That a triumph should be held in a foreign city was unthinkable! That Antony should hold one in his own honor, without benefit of a decree from the Senate confirming the recording of his campaigns was a slap in the face of Roman policy. Rome was humiliated and insulted, and this was seen as a final and irreparable separation between Antony and his homeland. Antony seemed to have no intention of returning home to share the sweetness of his accomplishments with the people of Rome, and Octavia had hoped that the conclusion of the war would bring her husband back, she was sorely disappointed. Her brother, Octavian, while no doubt shocked at Antony's unprecedented behavior and rebuffing of Rome, was now in an even stronger position than ever. The Pro-Octavian factions spared no effort or propaganda to play up the anti-Rome aspects of Antony's acts.

The triumphal procession weaved through Alexandria carrying the spoils of war – the Armenian treasure and various captured artifacts.

The triumph included the parading of prisoners of war through the streets of Alexandria. Prominent in their number were the King of Armenia and his family. The prisoners were ordered to march through the streets of the city, past throngs of onlookers, until they reached one of the city's central squares. There sat Cleopatra upon a gold and silver gilded throne, dressed as the Goddess

Isis. The Armenian royal family was commanded to bow down in front of Cleopatra and to worship her. The Armenians refused to accept Cleopatra's "divinity", and even Antony's severest threats did not convince them to kneel before her. The fear of being put to death as punishment did not cause them to bend a knee. Cleopatra was impressed by the Armenian King's refinement and pride, and in the end Antony spared them, although they remained in Egypt as state prisoners. It is generally agreed that the Armenian prisoners of war received far gentler and more humane treatment in Alexandria than they would have in Rome, or if Octavian had been their captor rather than Antony.

● **Donations of Alexandria** ●

The public in Rome was now set firmly against Antony, and their hatred for Cleopatra knew no bounds. Antony's love for and desire to please the oriental queen had deprived them of their celebration days of games and feasts. What was rightfully theirs was enjoyed instead by the Egyptian people. Antony had as much as declared that Alexandria was now the capital of his empire, and Rome had taken a back seat in his world. Cleopatra's dream for Egypt seemed to have been realized. The Romans, already jealous of Alexandria's beauty and richness, its broad streets, its port and lighthouse, now had even more reason to fear that it would indeed become the world's most influential city.

The triumphal festivities came to an end, but were followed quickly with an event that angered Rome even more, and pointed unwaveringly at Antony's steadfast devotion to Cleopatra and his adoption of Egypt and the East. Only a few days had passed during which the world could absorb what had already taken place, when another major pageant took place in Alexandria. A huge crowd gathered at the Gymnasium, near the mausoleum of Alexander the Great. Cleopatra and Antony sat upon golden thrones and regarded the gathering throng dressed as the God and Goddess Dionysus and Isis.

Situated below them on various levels height were the children. Thirteen year old Caesarion sat upon a gilded throne of his own, one step below his mother and the Triumvir, Alexander Helios and Cleopatra Selene, Antony and Cleopatra's six year old twins, sat on smaller golden thrones one

step below their brother. The youngest child, Ptolemy Philadelphus sat on a tiny throne at the lowest level. The children were dressed in a most curious manner. Alexander Helios wore the costume of Media, and the tiny Ptolemy Philadelphus wore the robes of a Macedonian King.

Antony rose to loudly and forcefully address the crowd, and what he said constituted the final undeniable break with Rome. The Eastern Empire was being declared as a separate and distinct entity, apart from Octavian's Roman Empire. Alexandria would indeed be its capital, and the family which sat upon this dais would constitute the beginning of its ruling dynasty.

The crowd listened raptly as Antony spoke. Cleopatra was declared Queen of Kings, and Queen of Egypt, Cyprus, Libya, and Southern Syria. Antony even called Cleopatra "wife of the great Caesar". Antony then turned to Caesarion, and solemnly recognizing him as the son of the great imperator, declared him co-regent with his mother, giving him the title King of Kings. Next, Antony bestowed upon Alexander Helios the monarchies of Armenia and Media and all of the countries in the Parthian Empire (which still remained to be conquered!) Cleopatra Selene was given rule of the territories east of Egypt still under Antony's control. The toddler Ptolemy Philadelphus was presented with Northern Syria and Sicily.

The reaction in Rome to these proclamations was severe. Antony had presented large portions of the empire to foreign princes, having conferred only with a foreign Queen. Using the children was a transparent ploy, and Antony's division of the empire was tantamount to a present to Cleopatra, naming her great queen of the East, and Alexandria capital. Antony's recognition of Caesarion as Caesar's son and heir was the icing on the bitter cake the whole spectacle constituted for Octavian, adopted son of the dictator, whom this threatened and insulted.

The year was 34 B.C., and Cleopatra's fondest dream had come true. She was Queen of Kings, ruler of a vast territories and mother of a dynasty. She must have felt extremely gratified that day upon the throne as Antony spoke so vehemently to her people. There can be little doubt that the entire script for this performance had been directed by Cleopatra herself, and Antony had put his stamp to it in great part to please her. This certainly did not escape notice in Rome where hatred of Cleopatra was had reached an all time high.

• Propaganda and Preparation •

During the two years following the establishment of Antony's eastern empire, Rome prepared for the final confrontation. It seemed abundantly obvious to them that Antony's intention was a final bid for total power, his sights set on becoming supreme ruler as Caesar had been. Cleopatra was seen as the instigator and enabler of this plan, and her control over Antony was so resented in Rome that she became the main object of their anti-eastern frenzy. That a mere woman, an Oriental Queen, could have such a heavy hand in affairs of the mighty Roman Empire was inexcusable and would not be countenanced. Octavian and his followers launched an energetic and successful propaganda war against Cleopatra which stirred emotions against her into unprecedented hostility.

Meanwhile Octavian made sure to get strong military footholds in all areas from which Antony could hope to invade Italy, should it come to that. He made internal improvements in Rome which were popular with the people, giving them hope that their city could still compete with the wonders that Alexandria possessed. Politically he also took pains to shore up his own image and besmirch that if Antony, attacking and criticizing him from the floor of the Senate. When Antony got wind of Octavian's public verbal attacks he dispatched a letter to the affect that he was surprised at Octavian's change of attitude, and if it was brought about because of his copulating with the Egyptian Queen then Octavian should realize it was only natural he should treat Cleopatra as he did, since she was after all his wife!

Octavian must have been mortified at such an outright declaration, since Antony's legal Roman wife was his sister, but the letter went on to further incite Octavian. Bringing up past liaisons with various women, Antony pointed out to Octavian that he was himself anything but the faithful and pure lad he seemed to demand that Antony be! He even brought up homosexual escapades and accused him of having tried to seduce Caesar! The propaganda war raged, as each tried to besmirch the other's character more successfully.

While the Roman masses seemed to side with Octavian, it was more out of fear and resentment of Cleopatra than out of antipathy toward Antony. The ruling classes in Rome and the two present consuls in fact still supported Antony. Octavian dealt with the hostility toward him in the Senate by having his supporters carry unconcealed weapons while he spoke passionately about Antony's transgressions, stirring up the senators by reminding them of the Donations and the Alexandria

… in order to put the curs'd monster
   in chains.
Yet she,
Seeking to die more nobly, showed
No womanish fear of the sword nor
   retired
with her fleet to uncharted shores.

Her face serene, she courageously
   viewed
her fallen palace. With fortitude
she handled fierce snakes, her
   corporeal
frame drank in their venom:

resolved for death, she was brave
   indeed.
She was no docile woman but truly
   scorned
to be taken away in her enemy's
   ships,
deposed, to an overweening
   Triumph.

Horace, Nunc Est Bibendum, Ode, Book I, 37, 1st century BC

triumph. The majority of the senators sided with Octavian, and the consuls and two hundred other senators who supported Antony all fled to the East to join him.

It was clear that the final confrontation was soon in the offing between Octavian and the West, and Antony and Cleopatra in the East. The year 33 B.C. saw both sides considering strategy and building forces for the inevitable showdown. Antony gathered his forces, mustered from all of his eastern allies, in Ephesus. When the fleeing Romans joined him, they were impressed by the armies Antony had managed to raise, but at the same time they were dismayed by the major role being played by Cleopatra, who had come to Ephesus along with a hefty Egyptian naval fleet. Even Antony's staunchest supporters were surprised at the way Cleopatra took part in every military consultation, and every political and strategic discussion. Antony was advised to send her back to Egypt forthwith, and the senators kept him apprised as to the anti-Cleopatra fervor in Rome. They were partly successful in their arguments, and Antony did promise to send Cleopatra back home when he realized that her presence played into Octavian's hand. However, when it came time to keep this promise, Antony apparently felt he could no longer function fully without the Queen at his side. He had grown dependent on her in every way, and in this critical time he simply could not do without her! Whereas Caesar had perhaps enjoyed her company and appreciated her intellect, Antony was completely overtaken by her and in service to her rather than the other way around. Cleopatra remained at Antony's side, to his great relief, and to the considerable consternation of his Roman supporters who knew that Octavian could make excellent use of the Queen's presence by making her the main issue of the coming war. In fact, without Cleopatra's insistence on the necessity of war it may actually have been diverted altogether since at one point Antony had suggested reconciliation to Octavian! The crafty Queen knew that without a final and

decisive victory for Antony her own throne and those of her children were not ensured. The dream of becoming Empress of Rome was still very much alive, and she made sure to keep Antony's ambition for total victory strong.

In early 32 B.C. Cleopatra finally succeeded in convincing Antony to send a formal divorce bill to Octavia. Even the senators who had joined him in the East agreed that the time was right for the dissolution of the marriage, and Octavia was duly ordered to vacate Antony's home in Rome. No single act could have demonstrated more clearly Antony's complete subordination to Cleopatra's wishes. It is reasonable to doubt that Cleopatra felt passionate love, or even deep affection for the aging Antony. At fifty-eight, Antony was showing signs of decline, whereas the thirty-nine year old Cleopatra was likely at the peak or her intellectual faculties and physical prowess. That she wished desperately to remain his mate is assuredly a fact, but that desire was born of her dream of power and glory, and not of want for domestic bliss with this man who was her inferior in so many ways. Cleopatra already anticipated the great victory of the Eastern forces over Octavian, and her own entry into Rome at Antony's side. It was unthinkable to her that at her shining moment she should ride into Rome as anything other Antony's legitimate and singular wife!

For Octavian, this humiliation of his sister and final and unnecessary demonstration of Antony's devotion to Cleopatra fanned the motivation to fight to even higher flames. Octavian, however, was reluctant to make

What of her who of late has put disgrace on us, and, a woman who fornicated even with her slaves, demanded as the price of her shameful union the walls of Rome and the senate made over to her dominion? ...to be sure, the harlot queen...

Sextus Propertius, Elegies, Book III, c. 24-22 BC

the first move, and he waited until late 32 B.C. for Antony to take a stand. Antony, on his part, was carefully building up his forces, while at the same time living a life of celebration, replete with all manner of entertainment and frolic. During the year before the war He took Cleopatra to Athens for her first glimpse of the city, and the two enjoyed ceremonies and pageants as the citizens of Greece paid homage to the Queen at Antony's bidding.

Rome watched as the hated Egyptian received accolades and cavorted in Greece sporting a bodyguard consisting of Roman soldiers with shields bearing her name. Cleopatra was determined to make a great showing of herself in Athens, as she was aware that her rival Octavia had previously been well-loved by the citizenry there. She was carried about the cities of Greece on a golden throne, while Antony followed on foot. At Antony's commission, a great statue of Cleopatra as the goddess Isis was erected next to his own at the Acropolis. Antony gifted Cleopatra with the library of Pergamus – still another generous and ostentatious gift. She remained at his side whenever possible, and then Antony was at meetings she did not attend, she would often have them interrupted by sending a note or love message which would be read out during the proceedings! These events were seen as more violations of Roman honor, and still more affirmations that Cleopatra was the woman behind the man, and the enemy to be ousted in war. Meanwhile, Cleopatra dispatched many works of art back to Alexandria, including various statues of Greek gods and sacred temple artifacts.

Antony still had friends in Rome, and they watched unhappily as things the Triumvir's reputation there went from bad to worse. In a last ditch effort to convince Antony to mend his ways and to send Cleopatra back to Alexandria, they sent an emissary, Geminius, to Greece. Geminius tried valiantly to gain Antony's ear and warn him of the imminent danger of his being ousted from

Roman office as a result of his behavior. Cleopatra understood immediately what Geminius' mission was, and undertook to have him humiliated at every

him at the end of the table at meals, and ordered her friends to tease and confuse him in conversation. Geminius bore these affronts patiently and waited for an opening, which came at a meal where Antony had imbibed a bit too much, and addressed the visitor, asking him to state his business. Before missing a beat, Geminius called out that he was there to entreat Antony to send his mistress packing back to Egypt immediately, before further damage could be done. Cleopatra was livid, but coolly stated that it was just as well that Geminius had let his mission be known without being tortured! When Geminius left Athens he was no longer among Antony's friends. What he had seen of Antony's subservience to the Egyptian Queen made him realize that the rumors circulating in Rome were true, and his support was then thrown to Octavian.

After a spat with Cleopatra, Plancus and Titius, Antony's supporters who had defected to him from Rome, could no longer abide the Queen or Antony's relationship with her. They switched their alliance, returned to Rome and went to Octavian, to whom they divulged the contents of Antony's will, which they knew would stir Roman emotions. Octavian wrested the will illegally from its guardians, the Vestal Virgins, and had it read publicly. Among the provisions of the will was a request that on his death Antony's body lie in state in Rome at the Forum, but that afterward it should be sent to Cleopatra, and buried in Egypt. That a Roman leader should wish to be buried on foreign soil was tantamount to his declaring his allegiance to another power. Burial in Alexandria meant adoption of Egypt as his home and the seat of his power.

● The War for the World is Declared ●

The final outrage had now been suffered by Octavian and Rome. Octavian now easily managed to convince the senate to strip Antony of his official powers. Rome then declared war on Cleopatra, Queen of Egypt. With this declaration, Octavian demonstrated his contempt and total loss of respect for his former brother-in-law. Not bothering to even to declare war on him directly, but only on Cleopatra. The basis for war was the Roman desire to liberate the lands Cleopatra had been given. Antony was not mentioned in the solemn declaration of war which took place in Rome along with the traditional ceremonies which accompanied such announcements. Once war was declared on the Queen, however, anyone on her side was de-facto an enemy of Rome. Thus, Rome was now finally and irrevocably at war with Antony.

This would be the war that could end the Roman Empire as it was known. The world watched breathlessly for the outcome. A victory by Antony would mean the rise of the East and its revenge upon its oppressors of hundreds of years. Should Octavian win, all of the Mediterranean countries would be under complete Roman rule. Octavian was loyal only to Rome, while Antony was led and motivated by Cleopatra. It was her fierce desire for the decisive battle to be fought, and her guidance and direction that drove Antony in his quest.

In early 31 B.C. Antony moved his infantry troops and his naval forces into Greece, concentrating his fleet at Actium. Octavian marched his armies eastward and stopped at the coast of Italy. Antony a larger naval fleet and a few thousand more foot soldiers. His advantage ended there, however, since in all ways other than numbers Octavian's forces were superior. Far more

capable and experienced, they had recently demonstrated military proficiency in other areas in the west over Sextus Pompey, whereas Antony's men were fresh from their defeat in the Parthian campaign. Octavian's ships were smaller, and more agile, making them more effective in battle than Antony's ponderous vessels. The Roman forces were also more organized and cohesive, and had the 'home advantage' of being near to their native land.

• Actium •

In the spring of 31 B.C. Antony had not yet formed any clear plan for an initiative, and Octavian stepped into the void. The Roman troops and naval fleet closed in on Antony's on the western coast of Greece. Octavian's second in command, Agrippa, was a brilliant strategist, and succeeded in making a first run at Antony successfully. During the spring of 31 B.C. Octavian's forces closed in on Antony's force until it was completely surrounded both on land and sea, and a blockade prevented supplies from being shipped to him. Antony suffered many losses, as well as a significant number of desertions by his troops due to lack of supplies, disease, and declining morale. Antony and his allies lost a string of battles, and the eastern forces were depressed and exhausted. A stalemate lasting into summer now hung over the combatants.

In the face of all this failure Antony began to show the weaker side of his character, and perhaps even to lose his ability to think clearly. He suspected Cleopatra of attempting to have him poisoned and detected treachery among friends and allies. For Antony to have been suspicious of the Queen points to the pressure and upset he must have been suffering. Cleopatra took the charge in her stride, and demonstrated her superior abilities at manipulation of Antony's thoughts and emotions. Rather than react with indignation and outrage, she simply planned the perfect protest which would show Antony that if she had wanted to do away with him she certainly could, but that her love was intact and could be trusted. Cleopatra put some poisonous herbs into a goblet which contained a drink for Antony. When she offered him the cup he did not hesitate to bring it to his lips. Cleopatra then stopped him, and to prove that she had 'saved his life' she ordered a prisoner to be brought to them and gave him the poisoned liquor. When the hapless prisoner immediately died, Antony understood the demonstration and his fear that his mistress was trying to murder him seemed to vanish.

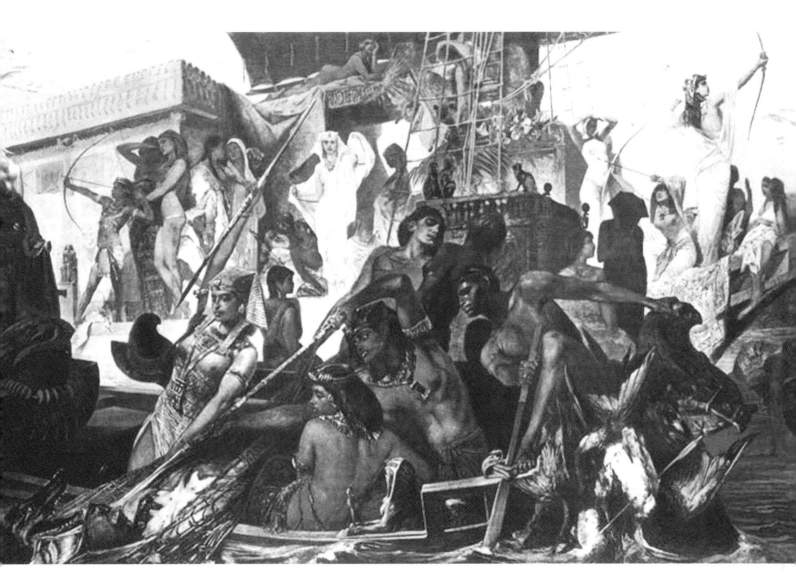

Disaster was in the offing and Antony was well aware of it. The stalemate would have to be broken, as Antony's troops were suffering greatly from the tight grip Octavian and Agrippa had managed to tie around his forces. By late summer Antony and Cleopatra were looking for ways to escape with at least part of their armies, and had all but abandoned any hope of conquest and victory. If only they could escape with their lives and preserve their empire in the east it would be enough!

Lacking a military adviser on par with Octavian's Agrippa, Antony turned to Cleopatra, upon whose advice he decided to make a decisive run past Octavian's navy. Antony knew he was running out of time. Many of his allies had defected to Octavian's side, and the blockade was causing what little morale his men had to deteriorate rapidly. Antony preferred to fight Octavian on land, where he felt more secure and experienced, but the latter shrewdly did not allow himself to be lured into a major skirmish, waiting instead for the inevitable show-down on the sea. Cleopatra, too, preferred a naval battle, and using her usual persuasive and seductive wiles, apparently convinced Antony that there was no choice. The Queen was aware that if they failed to make a clean break and escape Octavian's blockade, all was lost for her, but she did not entertain that possibility. When Antony called a Council of War to decide whether

Cleopatra, the shame of Egypt, the lascivious fury who was to become the bane of Rome...whose dangerous beauty...and the passions she aroused damaged our country greatly.

...it seemed possible that the world would be ruled by a woman, and not a Roman woman, either. Her insolence began on the night when she first gave herself to Caesar; it is easy to pardon Mark Antony's later infatuation when one remembers that she fired a heart so flinty as Caesar's.

to make their bid on land or sea, the council decided in favor of Cleopatra, and the fate of the Eastern Empire was sealed.

Antony took stock of his fleet and realized that he would be facing Octavian's four hundred small and quick ships with his own two hundred larger and stronger vessels. Antony disposed of his lesser ships by burning them. Cleopatra secreted her treasure on board her craft, amassing all of her gold and money to travel with her. Octavian caught wind of this, and determined to fight bitterly so as not to allow the Egyptian treasure to escape or go down with a ship!

The allied kings fighting with Antony were led to believe that the purpose of the upcoming battle was a victory over Octavian's navy, while secretly it was a bid for escape back to the east. It is not altogether clear whether the decision that all was already lost was made before the battle began, or if a signal was given later that a break for escape should be attempted. The fact that Antony sailed on September 2, 31 B.C. with all masts and sails raised and rigged points to his being set on making a run for it even then. The ships were clearly equipped for a long journey at sea, from which we conjecture that the plan was to run back to Egypt and wait for another confrontation there. Antony's fleet thus sailed forth at the outset rigged for flight, not for fighting!

Antony and Cleopatra sailed toward the gulf where Octavian was waiting for them. Antony's was the first of four squadrons, with Cleopatra's bringing up the rear. As they approached Octavian's navy,

She approached him in the manner of a suppliant, with a sorrowful face, but no resort to weeping, confident in her beauty. Though she pretended to tear her hair in grief, it was not sufficiently disarranged to lose its attraction. "Great Caesar," she said, "birth may count for little, yet I am still the Princess Cleopatra, a lineal descendant of King Lagus of Egypt. I have been driven from the throne, and shall never regain it without your help; which is why I, a queen, herewith stoop to kiss your feet. Oh, please become the bright star that blesses Egypt!..." Cleopatra would have stood no chance with the stern-hearted Caesar, but for the evil beauty of her face and person; she bribed her judge and wickedly spent the whole night with him...

Lucan, Civil War, Book X, c. 62 AD

Antony gave the order to his men to attack as though they were on land. Octavian's ships pretended to flee, turning out toward the open sea. When they had succeeded in luring Antony's fleet to follow, the fighting began in earnest. As the battle raged, the Egyptian battalion, which took no part in this clash, watched as Octavian's agile ships rammed at Antony's vessels, and retreated, repeatedly. They continued to watch as hand to hand combat took place when Antony's men succeeded in seizing the smaller Roman ships. A horrible and vicious battle seethed until the sea was littered with wrecked ships and bodies. Octavian's men fought with skill and strength and after several hours the tide turned in favor of the Roman forces. Cleopatra and the Egyptian fleet hung back and continued to take in the horrible sight, waiting for the opportune moment to make a break for it and flee back to Egypt. There can hardly be a doubt that this was the plan for her squadron from the beginning. When it looked as if Octavian's forces were clearly winning, Cleopatra's ships, rather than enter the fray and reinforce Antony's men, suddenly raised their sails and facing south, sailed speedily away. Some historians claim it is possible that Cleopatra's flight was preplanned but unknown to Antony, and that Cleopatra simply meant to desert him at his hour of need, and try to defect to Octavian later! Most agree, however, that the plan was bilateral, and that Antony was resigned in advance to losing the battle of Actium and escaping with his mistress, both of them to fight another day.

Antony observed the Egyptian fleet's leaving and immediately moved over to a smaller and faster ship, raised his flag, and sped off after Cleopatra. Left with no leader, the eastern forces soon capitulated to the Romans and the battle was over. The abandoned ships were captured, and most of the infantry forces surrendered and defected to Octavian. Octavian certainly won the Battle of Actium for Rome, but Antony did snatch a sort of victory by fleeing with an entire squadron and getting to safety himself.

● The Last Year ●

Octavian and some of his ships began to make chase after the fleeing enemy, but soon gave up the effort. Antony's small craft overtook Cleopatra's flagship along the coast of Greece, and bringing with him two of his trusted assistants, he transferred to deck of the Egyptian ship. Antony did not reunite with Cleopatra in celebration of their safety, nor did he commiserate with her about their defeat as might have been expected. Rather, he remained in solitary confinement on the bow of her ship for three days and nights as it sailed southward, silently hanging his head and wringing his hands in despair. He behaved as a man in the throes of deep shame and dejection. His armies were in total disarray and his fleet was lost. He had been trounced in a major skirmish, and had run away from the scene. It was almost more than he could bear, now that the reality of his situation had settled in his mind. While it certainly was not a surprise – he had known that he had no chance to win at Actium – now that it was over he sank into a hopeless depression, rousing himself only to give orders when the flagship was threatened by Liburnians, successfully driving them off.

We have to wonder what thoughts swirled in Antony's head during those three days. Did he wonder what might have happened had he not taken Cleopatra's advice and waged a sea battle against Octavian? What if he had heeded warnings and sent Cleopatra back to Egypt months beforehand? And if he had not fled the battle before it was over, and had ordered Cleopatra's battalion to back him up rather than make a run for it? Did Antony see himself for what he was – tied to a woman so strongly that he had lost the ability to think for himself?

And what of Cleopatra's thoughts during those first days of flight? Did she see Antony as a defeated appendage that could no longer be of use to her? Or did she rejoice in the fact that at least her lover had escaped with his life and they were together? Now that Octavian was the master of the Empire, what of Cleopatra's ambitions? Her future? Since her pattern was to align herself with the most powerful of men, perhaps this was the juncture when Antony ceased to be of interest – his appeal being commensurate only with his power. As they sailed for her home, she pondered how to save her throne and continue in power. Heavy thought indeed, but the Queen was far from ready to give up.

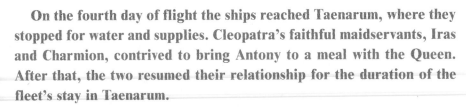

On the fourth day of flight the ships reached Taenarum, where they stopped for water and supplies. Cleopatra's faithful maidservants, Iras and Charmion, contrived to bring Antony to a meal with the Queen. After that, the two resumed their relationship for the duration of the fleet's stay in Taenarum.

When they set sail again, the ships pointed toward Egypt. Cleopatra wished to return home to Alexandria as quickly as possible of course, to reinstate herself on her throne before her people could get wind of the terrible defeat at Actium. Antony, however, could not face the thought of the Alexandrian's reaction when they heard of his defeat. Fearing stares and mockery, he decided to take refuge for the time being in Paretonium, where the ships next stopped for rest and water. His two faithful companions, Lucilius and Aristocrates remained with him. During the weeks they resided in Paretonium, news arrived that all of the Greek cities had heaped honors on the victorious Octavian, and that Antony's remaining legions had defected to Rome. Antony despaired of keeping the allegiance of the eastern provinces, and knew that he was reduced to having but one ally – Egypt. He once again plunged into anguish, and even contemplated taking his own life. Antony's nature would not allow that type of escape however, and even in the darkest moments his desire for life took precedence.

Cleopatra had by this time given up all illusions that Antony would be her key to power and glory. She probably had known for years that he was a shallow man with few outstanding personal virtues, but had stayed at his side in order to further her own lofty goals. Now, while sailing at full speed toward home, Antony was the farthest thing from her mind. She turned her considerable talents and strategic abilities toward preserving what was rightfully hers. Perhaps she even regretted that Antony did not have the courage to commit suicide and leave her to worry only about her own fate and that of her children.

As Cleopatra's fleet approached the harbor of Alexandria, the crew decorated the ships with wreaths, and belted out triumphant songs from the prows. Cleopatra sailed into her home port as if returning from a magnificent victory, not as a fugitive running for her life. Since the truth had not yet reached the Egyptian shores, the opposing party had no basis from which to seize power from Cleopatra, and she was not prevented from resuming her throne. She knew that there were many who would do her in at any opportunity, however, and at this juncture Cleopatra showed her capacity to be ruthless and cruel. Fear made her suspect Alexandria's leading citizens of planning to revolt, and she executed anyone whom she believed did not fully support her, filling her coffers with their treasure. Cleopatra ruled with firm command, and spared no opportunity to remind her subjects that she was still their Queen, descendant of the Ptolemies, and the deity Isis.

When Antony finally arrived in Alexandria, the Queen had little patience for his self-pitying mood. She would continue to strive as she always had. With an eye constantly to the future she refused to wallow in past defeat, or present humiliation. As long as there was a fight to be fought, Cleopatra schemed and planned to win it. This is not to say, however, that Cleopatra was unrealistic about her situation or what was likely to occur in the near future. She amassed her armies in Alexandria, gathering them from the outlying areas, planning to fight until the last in her home city when the inevitable showdown with Octavian should occur.

Antony repaired to solitary quarters off the Island of Pharos, where he continued to lick the wounds to his pride. The man who had conquered worlds and given kingdoms as gifts was now forced to stand by and watch as his bitter enemy swelled with honors showered upon him by those very kingdoms and provinces. While Cleopatra energetically faced the frightening future, Antony hid, perhaps afraid of assassination, or perhaps simply drained of will.

Caesar's favor was celebrated with a banquet, and a great fervor arose when she appeared in her full magnificence. Her banqueting hall was as large as a temple, and more luxurious than even our corrupt age could imitate. Its molded ceilings were embedded with precious stones, and its rafters were plated with gold. The walls were solid marble, pillars of agate supported the roof, and the entire palace had an onyx pavement. The great doorposts were solid ebony, the entrance was paneled in ivory, and its doors were inlaid with tortoiseshell – the dark patches covered by emeralds. There were jewel-studded couches, and rows of yellow jasper wine cups on the table. The palace staff was an assortment of old and young – some with black Numidian hair, some with such blond hair that Caesar had never seen the like before, some were Negroes. There was a group of unfortunate boys who had recently been castrated, and opposite them there was an older generation of eunuchs....

Into this scene stepped Herod, King of Judea. Seeing an opportune moment to get rid of the despised Cleopatra and perhaps, along with Antony, ingratiate himself with Octavian, Herod approached Antony with his idea. Since hatred and fear of Cleopatra had been the driving force behind Rome's declaration of war in the first place, perhaps the two of them should murder her, leaving the way open for reconciliation with Rome! Surely Rome would hale the hero who would rid the world of Cleopatra! Alas for Herod however, Cleopatra's power over the downed Triumvir was as intact as ever. Antony's love for the Queen and dependence upon her remained strong as always. Even a possible chance to escape his circumstances did not tempt him to do away with her. Eventually, Herod found another way to win over Octavian and join his camp.

Antony was abandoned now by the entire East, save Egypt. Cleopatra was indeed his only friend, and she continued to act loyal. If there was any small chance of preserving the Egyptian monarchy for herself and eventually for her son Caesarion, Cleopatra knew it would have to be through some sort of reconciliation between Antony and Octavian. True to her character and the robustness of her manipulative powers, she also had a back-up plan in this regard. Secretly, Cleopatra sent a messenger to Octavian bearing gifts from her – a scepter and crown, along with an offer of her kingdom in return for his pardon and allowing her children to inherit her throne. Some accounts report that Cleopatra actually tried

Cleopatra had added the finishing touches to an already fatal beauty by putting on so many wreaths and necklaces of Red Sea pearls that she panted under their weight…. The tables were rounds of citrus-wood, supported on gleaming elephant tusks – Caesar had never seen anything so fine…. Every variety of flesh, fowl, sea-fish or river-fish, every delicacy that extravagance, prompted not by hunger but by a mad love of ostentation, could bring from the ends of the earth, came served on golden dishes. Each guest received wreaths of flowering spikenard and perpetual roses, and the fresh oil of cinnamon which they poured on their hair had lost none of its fragrance in transit from the East.

Lucan, Civil War, Book X, c. 62

to seduce Octavian with words of love and affection – a tactic which had been so successful for her with men of power in the past. Octavian answered her publicly that her offer would be accepted if she would have Antony killed, or at the very least, denounced him and banished him from Egypt. Antony himself asked Octavian for the right to live as a private citizen in Athens, if not in Egypt. His request was not dignified with a reply. In subsequent offers, Antony begged for amnesty on the

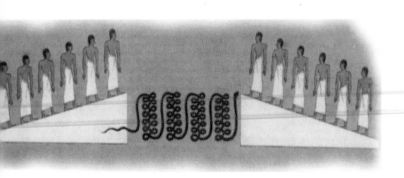

grounds that he and Octavian had familial ties. He argued that he should at least be afforded the destiny of Lepidus, the Triumvir who had, after being defeated by Octavian, been allowed to retire peacefully. These entreaties fell on deaf ears as well. Cleopatra ignored Octavian's counter-offer; probably knowing full well that even if she were to have Antony done away with Octavian would still march against Egypt and either put her to death or drag her back to Rome in chains.

Octavian perhaps read Cleopatra's lack of response as enduring loyalty toward Antony. He therefore took further effort to cause a rift between Antony and Cleopatra. An emissary named Thyrsus arrived in Alexandria and requested an audience with the Queen. Cleopatra afforded him an opportunity to state Octavian's offer again, and appeared to have been considering it, since she had several discussions with this fellow during which Antony was not present. It is doubtful that Cleopatra seriously entertained a plan to betray Antony as was suggested, and she was likely just humoring Octavian's representative. Antony, however, was incensed and upset and after a few days lost his patience with the intruder and had him hung and flogged. Cleopatra then tried to reassure Antony by courting him and paying him every attention, including a very elaborate birthday celebration.

• A New Society •

Cleopatra had lured Antony out of his island isolation for her own reasons of expediency, not out of longing for his company. While Antony and Cleopatra resumed cohabitation and to an extent their former pleasure-driven lives, instead of carousing happily as in previous times their frolics were now characterized by a cynical mood. Seeing themselves as doomed partners, they indeed had banquets and bouts of drunken revelry, but no longer called themselves the "Inimitable Livers' Society" as in the golden days of their early relationship. Cleopatra instituted a new society in its place - the "Companions in Death" whose members vowed to live and die together, come what may. Cleopatra was observed trying out poisons in methodical experiments on condemned prisoners noting which were the most efficient and dependable in securing a quick and clean death. Prisoner after prisoner as well as a number of animals died as the Queen honed in on the perfect poison and dose, noting the pain and agony suffered, and its duration and intensity. It was clear that Cleopatra was searching for the easiest way out of her earthly existence to be used when and if the point of no return arrived. She researched the method of death involving the least amount of time and physical pain, and settled, apparently, on the bite of a deadly asp, which caused its victims to fall into a deep sleep, from which they slipped quietly into death.

While she dabbled in the study of death, Cleopatra had clearly not yet given up hope that Octavian could be brought around to a reasonable settlement which would include leaving her kingdom and her children's birthright intact. First and foremost, she understood the importance of softening her image in Rome. If their hate and fear for her would abate, she reasoned, perhaps she could make inroads with Octavian and preserve the Egyptian throne for her children. Toward this end, The Queen staged an elaborate "coming of age" celebration for her son Caesarion, playing up the fact that the boy was a Roman - the son of Caesar, no less. She hoped to impress

upon Rome that the future leader would be male, and that she herself would gradually step down. The ceremony was carried out according to Roman tradition, with the seventeen year old Caesarion donning the toga of a grown man. Although carried out with a desire to win Roman affection for herself and her son, this act backfired and its effect was to condemn poor Caesarion to even more certain death. With his adoptive brother having been declared an adult, Octavian felt even more threatened. And playing up the boy's kinship to Caesar could only have fueled his resentment.

While Caesarion's festive birthday seemed to point to a forward looking attitude on the part of Cleopatra, her other pursuits at the time were of a nature more in tune with the poison experiments. She oversaw the construction of a mausoleum which would, according to tradition, house her remains when the time came. Rather than leave it empty however, the Queen ordered her treasure be transferred to the new structure. The entire Ptolemy treasure, including objects of gold, silver, emerald and pearl, as well as numerous statues and other works of art, were secured inside the mausoleum, which was built in Alexandria, alongside a Temple of Isis that was also newly erected. Stored with the treasure were enough torches and combustible material to allow Cleopatra to destroy it all at the last moment should the enemy close in on her. Cleopatra would not abide the thought of allowing Octavian to enjoy her riches after she was gone!

And so Cleopatra spent the last months of her life. She was a woman torn between action taken in hope and action taken in despair. Until the last, she desperately hoped for some kind of reconciliation with Octavian which would save her dreams for herself and her children. Her dreams of being the Empress of Rome were shattered, but she refused to believe that events had turned so wrong that she was to be the last Ptolemy monarch. Would she sacrifice Antony to assure an ending to the story in which she maintained her kingdom? All evidence points to the answer being yes. Whatever affection or even love Cleopatra may have had in her heart for her powerful lovers always played second to her love of power and glory and her fierce feeling of propriety over the throne of Egypt.

• The End Approaches •

A year passed after the battle of Actium. Octavian's armies were amassed to both the east and west of Egypt. Octavian was quite distressed when word reached him that the Queen had stored her treasure away and intended to destroy it should he advance on Alexandria. His intention had always been to make good use of the Ptolemy fortune and he wished to capture the Queen alive, not to afford her a dramatic exit before his triumph. Believing it might stop her from desperate action, Octavian sent messages hinting that he had fallen in love with Cleopatra and would certainly spare her life and her throne if Antony died. Cleopatra did not find this declaration of passion to be spurious and she eagerly sent word to Octavian that she accepted his romantic advances, believing she had finally succeeded in securing her throne. She was inclined at this point to call off her armies and acquiesce to Octavian, even though she knew full well that the latter would do away with Antony forthwith. Antony had become suspicious that the Queen had defected, but Cleopatra kept the cloak of secrecy around her dealings with Octavian. Antony, meanwhile tried to keep fighting, and led his troops against Octavian at Canopus, where his cavalry succeeded in routing Octavian's horsemen, in what was to be his final military victory.

Was Cleopatra Black?

For over two thousand years Cleopatra has been a mystery, an enigma, and a source of curiosity for writers and historians, scholars and school children. Only relatively recently, however, has the question of her racial identity become a popular one for debate. The African-American community in particular would like to claim Cleopatra as a "sister", and it's really no wonder that they play up her possible African genes. What group wouldn't be proud of having such a strong, intelligent, savvy, and powerful female figure in their history? But what are the facts? Unfortunately, there are not enough of them to prove beyond a doubt that Cleopatra was or was not an African Egyptian. We know that her father was Greek on his paternal side, but that he was the son of the previous Ptolemy Pharoah by an unknown woman. Until then, the Ptolemy line had been pure

Antony was cheered by this bit of success, and hurried back to Alexandria to share his pleasure with Cleopatra even though in his heart he must have known of her treachery. When Antony tried subsequently to go on the offensive against Octavian's armies there was very little actual fighting since his cavalry troops, his infantry, and finally his naval fleet, all went over to Octavian, apparently at Cleopatra's behest, or simply because they knew well enough that their situation was completely without hope. Antony cried out at this mass betrayal and cursed Cleopatra for her underhandedness, but even this did not dampen his passion for the Queen or reduce his loyalty to her.

Antony understood that all was lost. Octavian's armies were at the gates of the city, which lay defenseless and open. The citizens of Alexandria were paralyzed with fear of the imminent barrage of the Roman armies. And still Antony thought of Cleopatra. After all the disaster she had wrought on his life, all the wrong turns he had taken on her advice, he was still bewitched by her charms, and wanted to be with her until his last breath. On the night before the final invasion, Antony ordered a banquet be served in the palace. It was to be the final event celebrated by the "Companions in Death Society". Antony beseeched all present to eat and drink their fill, for tomorrow their city would surely have a new master.

Cleopatra, as we have said, was motivated by the same desires and ambitions as always up until her last breath. The Queen did not attend the final meeting of the "society". She was occupied with thoughts of her

Macedonian Greek. Auletes' mother, Cleopatra's grandmother, was likely a concubine in the Ptolemy court. No record exists of her appearance, so the possibility is open that she was a dark skinned African woman. History has likewise not revealed to us the identity of Cleopatra's mother – the woman who bore three and possibly four children to Ptolemy Auletes. She too, may have been a woman of the court, and possibly of pure African origin.

final desperate attempts at salvaging the situation. The teenaged Caesarion was sent out of Egypt with one of his tutors, in hopes this would keep him out of Octavian's clutches until and if she could negotiate for his security. She knew her only smidgen of hope to secure her throne and her children's inheritance lay in keeping her part of the deadly bargain with Octavian. Antony would have to be put to death, and soon. There was no other hope. Antony's demise was the only tiny ray of hope of life for Cleopatra, and she knew she must follow it. Even at this final desperate hour, Cleopatra controlled Antony by virtue of his affection for her and she conceived a plan by which she was sure Antony would take care of the horrendous deed for her! She reasoned that Antony would never be able to face life without her, and that upon hearing that she was dead, he would surely fall upon his sword in grief!

Cleopatra took her handmaidens, Eris and Charmian, and the three of them barricaded themselves in the freshly built mausoleum. Antony was duly notified that the Queen had taken her own life, and she waited anxiously for word that he had indeed put an end to himself. Antony received the news with shock, and was beside himself with despair. Although he had suffered enormous defeats and disappointments in the past several years, and had several times been close to suicide, this news was more than he could bear, and he ordered the nearest slave to stab and kill him. He removed his breastplate, and set it down declaring that he would now be reunited with the Queen, therefore there was no reason for sadness. His only regret, he said, was to have been of lesser courage than a woman. The slave raised his sword, but unable to pierce his master's heart, he fell upon it himself. Antony then grabbed up his own weapon

Cleopatra was the first of the Pharoah's to learn the Egyptian language and to identify herself closely with the Egyptian culture. Perhaps this is evidence of her mother's or grandmother's influence.

None of the Roman historians who recorded events of her time saw fit to mention anything notable about Cleopatra's race or color, and one might assume they would have done so had she been a full Black Egyptian, and thus different from her predecessors.

Several images of Cleopatra have been preserved through the centuries on coins and busts. Obviously we cannot tell skin color from these, and have to make do with the shape of her features. Cleopatra was not a raving beauty, and neither was she a plain Jane. Her features were strong and even, her nose perhaps a bit imposing.

So was she "Black"? The answer: Maybe. We'll never know for sure.

———◆———

and shouting his thanks to the slave for showing him what needed to be done, he plunged the blade deep into his chest, falling to the ground bleeding and in agony. His stabbing missed his heart however, and he wounded himself severely in the stomach. Antony lost consciousness, but after a while during which observers probably took him for dead, he revived. When he realized that death had not come immediately Antony begged his companions to finish the job for him, but they refused, and ran from his presence in terror.

Cleopatra was brought the news that although Antony had tried to end his own life, he had not succeeded. Somehow Antony too was notified that the Queen was still alive, and he demanded to be taken to her. Slaves bore the bleeding man, whose life was ebbing away, to the door of the mausoleum, but Cleopatra, fearing that Octavian's soldiers could appear at any moment, refused to open it. The entry remained blocked by huge slabs of stone. Bystanders, along with Cleopatra's handmaidens, attached a pulley and ropes to Antony's gurney, and with great effort hoisted Antony up and into the mausoleum through an unfinished portion at the top. This feat was most taxing and difficult as Antony was not a small man, and it took some time, precious minutes of the last hour of Antony's life. We don't know how Cleopatra felt about being reunited with Antony as this moment – there are conflicting reports. Some accounts claim that Cleopatra fell on him with love and grief, tearing at her garments, smearing her face with his blood, and beating her breast with sorrow. Antony is said to have declared that he regretted nothing and had lived a happy life. Others claim that this is unlikely, and that Cleopatra allowed Antony entry to the mausoleum only so that she could take credit for his death when finally Octavian confronted her. Antony reportedly used his last breath to tell Cleopatra that she must try to reconcile with Octavian and save herself. He mentioned one of Octavian's men, Proculeius, explaining to Cleopatra that he alone among the Romans could be trusted and that Cleopatra should try to negotiate through him for safe deliverance. Antony requested a sip of wine, and beseeched Cleopatra not to mourn for him, but to rejoice in the good they had shared. Then he died in her arms.

• Cleopatra's Last Stand •

Messengers lost no time informing Octavian that Antony's life was over. One was dispatched by Cleopatra, and another was a member of Antony's bodyguard who brought Octavian the bloody sword, and reported that Cleopatra remained within the mausoleum with her treasure. The news was met first with jubilation in Octavian's camp. Almost immediately, however, Octavian switched to the role of mourning friend and sibling. Fashioning his reaction after Caesar's when he had been presented with the head of the fallen Pompey, Octavian wished to be seen as just as compassionate. He now repaired to his tent to observe a period of mourning, before dealing with the Queen.

Octavian had no intention of allowing Cleopatra to set her fortune ablaze, herself along with it. He was determined to have her led through the streets in chains at his triumph in Rome. Octavian set about now to convince Cleopatra that he meant to treat her with lenience and understanding, lest she take matters into her own hands. He sent two emissaries, Gallus and Proculeius, to Cleopatra's tomb. Conversing through the great boulders at the entrance, they discussed the Queen's children and what was to become of them. Cleopatra begged that they be left alive to inherit the kingdom which was their legacy. As Gallus attempted to reassure her that Octavian meant no harm to her family and could be trusted in all matters, Proculeius, the man Antony had told her could be trusted, made his way with some soldiers to the back of the mausoleum where they quietly climbed ladders to the unfinished portion through which Antony had earlier entered.

They bounded into the quarters where Antony lay in a pool of blood, and past him to the front entrance where they found the Queen and her handmaidens deep in conversation with Gallus through the heavy portals. When Cleopatra heard the soldiers declare her prisoner, she snatched a knife from her robes and attempted to dash it into her breast. Proculeius was upon her in a heartbeat, forcing her arms behind her and the dagger to fall to the floor. Cleopatra was helpless to escape the knowledge of what had happened to her. The vast Ptolemy treasure which she had so painstakingly amassed in the mausoleum was now in Octavian's hands, as was she. The soldiers removed Antony's body from the mausoleum and put the Queen and her handmaidens under guard in an upper room of the structure. They were thoroughly searched for concealed poison and weapons.

How Did Cleopatra Die?

Popular legend has it that Cleopatra died from the bite of an "asp". When we examine this proposition however, we see that it is quite improbable. There does exist a venomous asp (Vipera Aspis), and it is quite an aggressive snake. It can be found in the mountains of Europe, and has caused several deaths in France. However, the asp is a slow moving animal whose bite is not always fatal, and whose venom takes time to cause pain and other symptoms. The most impressive reason for doubting it's culpability in the death of the Queen is that the asp is not indigenous to Egypt, and never has been in the past. Therefore, if Cleopatra was killed by a serpent, it is almost certain that it was not an actual asp. More likely, the word asp has been used over the years as a sort of generic term for snake. If we assume that the suicide weapon was a snake of some sort, the most logical candidate for the job would have been the Egyptian cobra. Cleopatra studied long and hard in

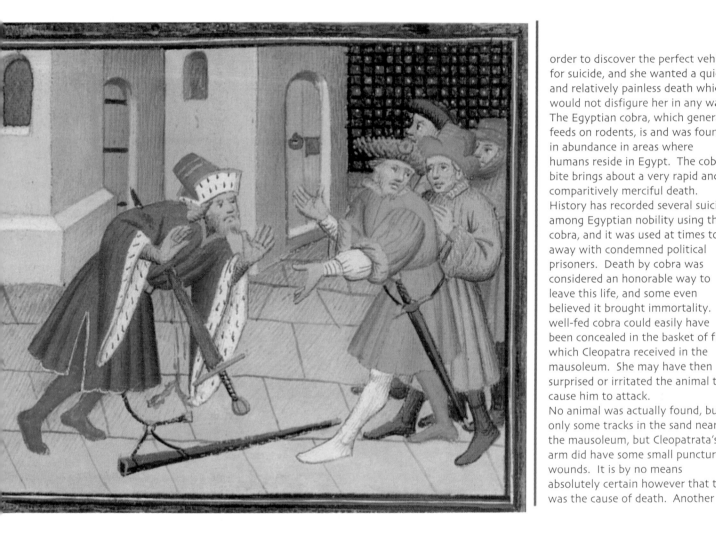

order to discover the perfect vehicle for suicide, and she wanted a quick and relatively painless death which would not disfigure her in any way. The Egyptian cobra, which generally feeds on rodents, is and was found in abundance in areas where humans reside in Egypt. The cobra's bite brings about a very rapid and comparitively merciful death. History has recorded several suicides among Egyptian nobility using the cobra, and it was used at times to do away with condemned political prisoners. Death by cobra was considered an honorable way to leave this life, and some even believed it brought immortality. A well-fed cobra could easily have been concealed in the basket of figs which Cleopatra received in the mausoleum. She may have then surprised or irritated the animal to cause him to attack.

No animal was actually found, but only some tracks in the sand near the mausoleum, but Cleopatrata's arm did have some small puncture wounds. It is by no means absolutely certain however that this was the cause of death. Another

Octavian's army advanced into Alexandria, and at every turn reassured the people that they were to be well treated and in no way held accountable for the wars their Queen had forced upon them. He allowed no looting and ordered his soldiers to treat the city with respect and honor. Octavian and his party took over the royal palace, from which he directed the takeover of the city. A party was sent out to retrieve

theory holds that the Queen's handmaidens had a potent poison hidden in their hollow hair pins which they administered to her. Also unknown for certain is how the handmaidens themselves expired. Family Ties: Incest Among the Ptolemies

To the modern reader, one of the most striking features of Ptolemaic royal life was the ubiquitousness of first and second degree incestuous marriage. That the incest was practiced as a matter of course and with no accompanying comment or justification points to it being an acceptable form of behavior for the times. In Rome, marriage among full siblings was in fact prohibited by law, but half siblings could wed. In Egypt even brother-sister and parent-child marriages were allowed. So the fact that the Ptolemies married one another almost exclusively hardly made a ripple in the consciousness of the times.

There was good reason from the Pharaohs' point of view to marry within the family. Since everything of value was passed down through families, each succeeding generation desired to keep the family fortune

for itself, and limited leakage of the dynasty's treasure and power to outsiders. Let us not forget, too, that the Ptolemy's considered themselves close to gods, and many of them actually identified themselves as deities. Would a god marry a mortal? Not if there was a proper god to marry. The nearest pure deified member of the opposite sex was often a sibling. During the entire 200 year reign of the Ptolemy dynasty, incestuous marriage was the norm, and the pharaohs married outside the family only when there was no suitable mate within it. And "suitable" would cover a wide range – it seemed any member of the family of the opposite sex, no matter what their age, could be chosen.

That these marriages included sexual relations, and were not just marriages of legality and

convenience, is certain. The Ptolemy line bore offspring from almost every union. (Cleopatra's two marriages to her child-brothers are exceptions) Love, however, is certainly another question. Did the Ptolemy marriages include any form of affection or even respect? Perhaps in some cases, though the norm would seem to point to a resounding no. Cleopatra's own two marriages to her much younger brothers both ended in the deaths of

Caesarion and his companion from their flight. The younger twins were ordered sent back to Rome where Octavian would adopt them and see to their upbringing.

Octavian continued to make efforts to seem magnanimous, and announced his intention to allow Cleopatra to give Antony a burial as she saw fit. Cleopatra and her servants spent several days embalming Antony's body in the mausoleum, and an elaborate burial was staged nearby. Cleopatra's display of grief was severe and unrelenting. She beat her breasts and wailed and moaned inconsolably. We can only surmise that she grieved not only for Antony but for Egypt – for she had by now lost absolutely everything which had ever been of any consequence to her, and her despair undoubtedly knew no bounds.

After burying Antony Cleopatra fell ill with fever and infection, perhaps caused by the self inflicted wounds to her breasts. Having lost all will to live, the Queen welcomed her ailments as an excuse to give up and

the unfortunate youths, one because he was inconvenient, and the other because he had become the enemy. Ptolemy IX, on the other hand, supposedly had strong feelings for his wife and sister Cleopatra IV.

From our vantage point it is often wondered how the Ptolemies seemed to maintain excellent vigor of mind and body, when modern medicine insists that inbreeding causes various and serious physical defects. Experiments with animals have shown repeatedly that the inbred stock suffers small stature, weakness of constitution and a propensity to disease, to say nothing of the high likelihood of mental retardation, all within a relatively short span of several generations. There is no ready explanation for why these afflictions did not seem to affect the Egyptian royals. Cleopatra herself of course had "outside" blood in her veins, since both grandmother and probably her mother were not from the Ptolemy line.

allow her body to afford her escape from unbearable reality. She stopped taking nourishment and waited for death to claim her weak and ravished body. Octavian would not hear of allowing the Queen to starve herself at this late date, and he sent word to her that if she continued in her hunger strike the young Ptolemy and Cleopatra Selene would be put to death. At this threat Cleopatra rallied, began to take food, and regained some of her strength. She was attended by her handmaidens and doctors and allowed to recover at the palace.

During her illness Cleopatra was paid a first visit by Octavian. Surprising her, he found the Queen lying unadorned and in disarray on a pallet, ill and aging. Octavian attempted to pacify her, showing compassion and even friendliness. His purpose now was only to get Cleopatra back to Rome so that he could parade her at his Triumph. This purpose was leaked to Cleopatra by Dolabella, one of Octavian's men who had developed a fondness for the Queen, and Cleopatra set about forging her final plot to "escape".

Cleopatra:
...I laughed him out of patience; and that night
I laughed him into patience; and next morn,
Ere the ninth hour, I drunk him to his bed;
Then put my tires[1] and mantles on him, whilst
I wore his sword Philippan[2].

1.headdress
2.Antony's sword is named after Philippi, where he conquered Brutus and Cassius)

From Shakespeare: Antony and Cleopatra Act 11, scene 5

• The End •

Octavian now believed he had deceived the Queen in to trusting that she would be leniently cared for, and when he received a request from her to visit Antony's grave he saw no reason it should not be granted. A month had passed since Antony's death, and Cleopatra begged to be able to make the customary offerings and prayers.

Cleopatra knew this would be her last chance to escape being humiliated in the Roman triumph. All was already completely lost. All, that is, but the Queen's sharp mind and will to leave life on her own terms. On the way to the gravesite Cleopatra spoke to the Roman soldiers who guarded her, giving them the impression that she was resigned to being dragged to Rome in chains and executed. She and her handmaidens approached Antony's tombstone, and performed a moving and heart wrenching memorial ceremony. Directly from the grave, Cleopatra's entourage moved to her mausoleum which stood nearby, and Octavian's soldiers stood guard as she entered along with Iras and Charmion. The maids bathed their mistress, and dressed her carefully in royal robes, adorning her hair with the decorations of the Goddess Isis. Cleopatra then was offered a meal, which she consumed while reclining on a couch. What thoughts must she have entertained during this repast? Surely she thought of Caesarion, who by now she hoped had attained his escape, and of her younger children, whom Octavian had promised not to harm. Did she think of Egypt? Of Caesar? Perhaps she simply sipped wine and tried to think of nothing at all but blessed peace and escape from the trials and hardships of being the most powerful woman in the world.

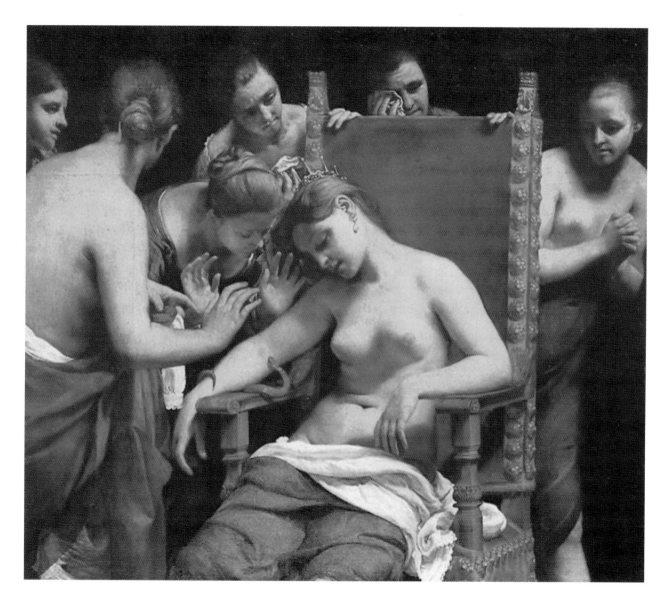

As the Queen dined, a man approached the heavily guarded entrance to the mausoleum bearing a basket of ripe figs. The guards were offered a taste, and satisfied that the offering was indeed only fruit they let the man enter the tomb to deliver it to Cleopatra. When the fruit arrived, the Queen prepared a written message requesting that she be buried with Antony, and dispatched it to Octavian. When the man who brought the fruit had left and the messenger had been sent, Cleopatra lay back on her couch, as her handmaidens adjusted her robes and diadem.

When Octavian received the message he knew at once what had happened and he sent soldiers to prevent the Queen from killing herself. When they arrived they found Cleopatra regally dressed and laid out on a royal bed, dead, with her handmaidens breathing their last labored breaths at her side.

Cleopatra the Great was dead at age 39. Octavian now ruled the world. The year was 30 B.C.